Holocaust
at
The Felling

By

Bernard W. Haugh

authorHOUSE™

1663 LIBERTY DRIVE, SUITE 200
BLOOMINGTON, INDIANA 47403
(800) 839-8640
WWW.AUTHORHOUSE.COM

First published by AuthorHouse 11/21/05

ISBN: 1-4208-7388-1 (sc)

Printed in the United States of America
Bloomington, Indiana

This book is printed on acid-free paper.

Dedicated to No. 92 and to all of the citizens of The Felling, past and present, which includes my parents, Rose and Joe, sister Moira and my wife Maureen whose unfailing support has been essential.

Table of Contents

Chapter 1 - The Holocaust

His shoulder ached abominably. Sitting there with Fenwick and looking down across the distant river on a bright but breezy late May morning the world seemed different, unreal - and painful. Not much more than an hour or so earlier, with the end of the morning shift in sight, a fall of stone in the new Felling colliery had all but buried him. Fenwick had pulled him clear and brought him, bewildered, up to the surface. Now they sat chatting on the steep slopes of the Tyne valley overlooking the large new busy colliery, observing the purposeful river traffic between Friars Goose and St. Anthony's backed by the soft southern lowlands of Northumberland tapering eastwards towards the river entrance and the sea.

Nothing appeared to be broken. He was taken home where his mother had washed out and tended the various cuts. For the first time he could remember, she had not dosed him with the ever-present *Gordon's Cordial* kept in the kitchen cupboard and he had resisted his father's view that the doctor be seen. The colliery owners had, to be fair to them, arrangements with doctors in the locality of their workings and also with the Keelmen's Hospital upriver at Newcastle, for surgery cases.

"You were lucky, really."

"Thanks."

"No, really. It was mainly one big boulder which must have knocked you to one side as it came down, and the other stuff probably hit and covered you before Long Tom and some of the Gateshead lads helped get you out. I remember one time when half a mast got shot away and hit the deck without seriously hurting anyone at all underneath. Quite a few got cut and bruised though in all the tangle of ropes and pulleys and falling spars."

"Well, thanks again for getting me out, Fenwick." Matt thought it best to say something at this point just in case his companion was inclined to get into one of his tales. Not that he told out and out untruths. It was just that to any ready or unsuspecting hearer his stories tended to be embellished only just within the bounds of possibility and his estimate of the listener's credulity. It was one of Fenwick's charms that he appeared forever to be unaware of the gradual and growing scepticism of his audience which, especially if non sea-fairing, was generally too polite to respond with blank disbelief. When anyone did, there was usually someone to whom he would appeal and get guarded tolerant support.

Matt was sixteen and about three years younger than Fenwick, who was a relative on his mother's side of the family and who had certainly served at Trafalgar. Several years later he had returned home with some money, largely his share of the government's miserly bounty. The deflected anecdote was doubtless another in a long line supporting his apparent lifetime thesis that the historic battle had been won with all due respect to Nelson and Collingwood, of course, but mainly by Fenwick.

"What was that?"

"What?"

The very ground they were sitting on shivered. There was a low rumbling sound like distant gunfire causing them both to look downriver where navy boats might be tied up at Shields. The skies weren't right for thunder.

The next instant a roar and belch of orange and yellow flame shot out of the pit head below them, followed by a blast of coal dust, stones, splintered wood and general debris in a cloud rising above the John Pit workings and showering the surrounding farmland and cottages. They stood up, horrified, and started to move down towards the colliery and their home not far beyond.

They had covered no more than a few yards when a second explosion erupted with such a ferocity of heart-stopping primal noise they were first of all paralysed with fear and then both started in panic to scramble back up the bankies away from the inferno. Flames and debris now shot high into the air massively in excess of the first eruption and filled the skies with smoke, dust, burning embers and choking mephitic fumes which seemed to pour out of the bowels of hell itself. Mid-day turned to near nightfall such was the almost instant loss of light.

After a few moments of terrified clambering, their self-preservation was apparent despite the painful gasping of lungfulls of foul sulphurous air and the flaming smouldering missiles falling all around. Looking back, there were signs of people apprehensively moving behind cover and it could be seen that the engine house, not being directly over the pit shaft, had clearly survived.

"Come on, Matt." They now resumed their downward scramble both already regretting having turned tail in their personal terror. Workmates and locals were even now beginning to cluster in bewildered and apprehensive groups approaching the shaft, not knowing how to react but all fully aware that there was no one but themselves to help the plight of those stranded in the black depths below. As they got near, someone shouted "Water!" and a melee set to with buckets and water butts tackling the major and minor fires all around, grateful for an immediate focus for energetic action of some kind and all sickened with a fearful dread of what existed hundreds of feet beneath them, or didn't exist at all.

"Must be firedamp. Look, you go home and check that the folks are all right. The engine men think the shaft might be usable and they're going to try to get someone down there and lift any survivors out of it with ropes and sheer bloody manpower. The engine must have had it. They'll need better shoulders than yours at the moment hauling on the gin pulley."

Fenwick hurried over to the shaft head making his way past small groups and individuals busily and determinedly attending all manners of fires, large and not so large, caused by the incendiary fall out from the John Pit shaft. Noise and commotion everywhere.

"How many are down there?"

"Dunno. Perhaps a hundred, God help them. The back-shift had just gone down and the fore-shift were just about to come up. So it would be packed down there. Mind, a few had come up not long before the end of the shift."

"I know. There had been a fall and I came up with young Matt Robson and some others."

"Right. We've enough sound rope on the gin pulley but it's a six hundred-foot lift. Get on the end of that with as many men as you can find. The shaft smoke seems to be clearing so I'll go down first and see what needs to be done." Seemingly matter of fact the overman, Anderson, a very brave man who would have been surprised to have heard himself described as such, prepared to be lowered down the smoking but clearing shaft clutching his flint/steel mill, which would give him some light and help him to find out what he needed to know of conditions below.

"I'll come with you - and turn the mill," Fenwick added in persuasion.

Willing hands took the strain and lowered two very brave men into the smoke-wisped void. One of the hewers peered over the edge, signalling to the rope team and listening out for instructions from the men already out of sight, balancing on their rudimentary wooden cradle and watching out to protect themselves with their spare hands from the passing walls of the shaft sides. Anderson could see the bottom approaching and bellowed upwards for their descent to be slowed. They hit some of the debris of stonework and timbers at the bottom working level not too heavily and were greeted by workmates even more blackened and tattered than usual. Their rapturous welcome would have done justice to the Archangel Gabriel himself.

"Well. What fettle?"

"There's roof falls all over. Some bad injuries, especially yon little lads."

"Right. Put them in first, one at a time, along with somebody fit to help them both up. Quickly."

An eight or nine year old, barely conscious and clearly suffering from more than his all too evident flesh wounds, was tenderly placed in the crude cradle together with an older collier making light of his own head wound. He also had a badly crushed foot, but with two good arms he could offer some help and protection to them both in their upward journey.

Another bellowed instruction up the shaft, the rope jerked taught and the cradle and contents rapidly disappeared from the limited sight of those below. It returned with unexpected rapidity just a few moments later it seemed. Only a frantic last minute shouted warning prevented the precious cradle from crashing past them and hurtling into the confusion of rubble and wreckage strewn down in the well of the shaft bottom.

"Didn't think to mark the rope last time, did they?" In different circumstances Anderson might have shown some mildly amused exasperation but now he had too much on his mind. The shocked and bewildered men and boys who, incredibly, had somehow survived the holocaust took heart from Anderson's very presence and quickly fell to with remarkable and patient order in arranging pairings of the injured and able bodied or semi-able bodied for the priceless lifts to safety.

In well under an hour all thirty or so survivors found huddled around the bottom of the shaft had been lifted clear. The willing, torn hands, the aching shoulders hauling at bank on the lifting rope, the weary legs and sulphur-seared lungs could now rest. At the bottom of the shaft Anderson had established that any other survivors were beyond argument now sealed behind massive stone falls. No responses came in answer to their various hopeful hammerings on the obstructing stonework and he feared the already evident afterdamp, to be heard continuously issuing from hissing fissures and which would lie, accumulate and venomously ease out the remaining life-sustaining oxygen. Sparks from Fenwick's hand held mill fell like drops of crimson blood in the pockets of afterdamp and breathing was becoming more and more difficult. "Let's go," he murmured after a wordless pensive while, not daring to clarify his thoughts, even to himself.

They clambered into their crude but priceless container.

"Haul away."

At the top of the shaft intense emotions of anxiety, relief, euphoria and despair had greeted every returning precious cargo. Feelings of relief and gratitude as close relatives and friends were helped to safety and reunited were quickly followed by mixed feelings of guilt and anguish, as it became apparent that no more could be saved immediately. For most of those gathered around the pithead in a common bond of numbed fearful foreboding it was soon apparent the increasing probability was that the future was likely to hold little but agonisingly painful and conclusive news and lives changed forever.

Dr. Thornton had arrived in his pony and trap and, sleeves rolled up and face set in a grim preoccupied frown, had set up his base for operations in the store room next to the stables. The animals were twitchy and wild eyed but becoming pacified after their initial terrifying experiences so close to the roaring, flaming John Pit shaft. Almost the first of the good doctor's ministrations was to tend the worst of the kicks and bruises the stablemen and boys had collected trying to bring order out of chaos among the wildly panicking and rearing horses and ponies. The customary atmosphere of the store room, a dry pervasive smell of oatmeal backed by an underlying and unmistakable aroma of horse manure, soon acquired strong elements of sulphur, various pungent liniments and tobacco.

As the injured survivors, some of them very badly injured, were brought to him he was soon swamped with the demand for his attention. He sensibly selected various of the walking wounded and gave directions for suitable treatments to be carried out by their families at home. Eyes were rinsed of coal dust, limbs rough washed for the inspection of bruises and contusions, in case more serious injuries lay beneath. Rough and ready tourniquets were applied with some success. His calming presence gave reassurance to those uncontrollably shaking with the after effects of shock. He struggled on, velvet-collared jacket off and un-buttoned sleeves rolled up, in these most basic and sparse of conditions having little more than the tools of his trade which normally accompanied him in his trap, to keep pace with the urgent needs of the blackened, bloodied, broken and damaged bodies now being brought to him by the minute.

Into the afternoon, the waiting crowd grew in motley numbers and pensive tearful wailing anxiety gave way to subdued chatter punctuated with heartbroken sobs and raised voices questing for some sort of action, almost any action, to break the frustration of inactivity and to offer some hope of further rescues.

There was a further blinding flash of yellow flame from the shaft and a gush of debris came out with a roar, which scattered the crowd with terrified shrieks and bewildered curses. Fortunately, it was only some sort of dramatic but brief after-blow. The colliers in the crowd quickly returned to find out the fate of Anderson and those who had joined him in a second descent to check the conditions around the shaft bottom and assess the prospects of mounting further rescue attempts to release those trapped behind the many massive roof falls.

As the cloudy blackness cleared their hopefully directed cry of "Hullo" down the shaft was returned with a distant but positive "Hullo" in return, which galvanised everyone into a speedy check of the rope and cradle before lowering away and hauling up once again.

Anderson and Fenwick were last up. Anderson shook his head.

"Afterdamp, definitely. Lots of it near the shaft bottom and getting worse. No chance of doing anything down there now until it clears. We hammered again on the faces and sides of all of the roof falls. Not a sound of a reply anywhere."

He paused. Every face in front of him registered a look of hollow, anguished, beaten but understanding despair. Muffled sobs smothered into shawls. Men's eyes narrowed and cheekbones whitened under the coaldust. A horse whinnied, someone cursed. Some feet slowly turned and trudged quiet and subdued in the direction of devastated and traumatised homesteads, footprints making their outline in the fallen black dust, as in a fall of fine fresh snow. Many stayed where they were in their groups, disconsolate and bewildered, but determinedly reluctant to abandon hope.

Chapter 2 - Fenwick's Story

The Northumbrian coastline was familiar to Fenwick from as far back as he could remember. As a boy he had often sailed with his father, Seth, from the family home and business base in Blyth down to the Tyne and occasionally as far as Whitby. His father was an old deep sea mariner, once sailing with Cook but, not relishing any more long arduous and ever more unpredictable years far away from home waters, had returned to Blyth to set up a ship's maintenance and chandlery business on the strength of his skills as a ship's carpenter and his savings from years at sea.

Late in life then he had married the daughter of an old family friend. Her name was Mary Jane, at the time not seriously contemplating the prospect of marriage, herself an only child and into her forties. Fenwick then arrived somewhat unexpectedly, a lifelong characteristic. They were a hard working if unimaginative couple and cared for the boy as well as the expectations of their lives and times required. Certainly, his father telling of his years of seafaring gave Fenwick a growing interest and inclination towards sea-going ships and the life associated with them.

One particular boyhood trip to the Tyne made a big impression. When they sailed in and tied up at North Shields the harbour was dominated by a 74-gun ship of the line and two attending frigates. The frigates themselves were bigger than any vessel he had ever seen before and the 74 gunner easily dwarfed the dockside buildings outside of which he waited for his father to finish some of his business of the day. There were masts, ropes and barrels everywhere. Sails were being furled and unfurled. Ships were loading or unloading, repairing and cleaning. Doors and hatches were slamming. Men and boys were clambering over decks and rigging. There were shouts and whistles, orders were being barked from impressive uniforms and the whole dockside a bustle of voices with metal-rimmed wheels and horses hooves sharply ringing and clattering over the stone and cobbled paving.

He later recalled asking a friend of his father if the biggest of the ships would have fitted into Durham Cathedral.

"What sort of question is that, son?"

"Well, me ma says Durham Cathedral is the biggest building she's ever seen. Me da thinks it is too and he's been all over."

A month or more later, the same man came up to himself and his father and said, "I think that big warship would have fitted into the cathedral with its sails folded, but you might have had trouble getting it out through the door and sailing it down the

River Wear!" He remembered nodding sagely at this information, and wondering why the two men seemed to be so amused.

He was almost twelve when he decided to leave home. He bided his time for several weeks and watched out for a vessel headed for the Thames where the naval boats came from. He wanted one not planning to put in at any of the northern ports on its way south for fear that, after discovery, he might be off-loaded onto a northern bound local vessel or perhaps one of the red-sailed, brightly coloured hulled Whitby cobles. Then he would be returned home in shame and ignominy to face the wrath of his father and the despair of his mother.

It wasn't too difficult to get away. By this time he was well known around the harbour and to many of the crews. No one seeing him around would have taken much notice. There were plenty lads around his age and size working on the docks or, for that matter, in the vessels themselves. He hid among the cargo of his chosen escape craft, a medium-sized square rigged trader, and listened with mounting excitement while the crew prepared the vessel to get under way.

On his usual dockside spot the blind fiddler could be heard winding out his tunes, bantering by name with the local girls in anticipation of a copper or two in his hat from a passing sailor ever hoping to impress one of them. Orders were shouted out, ropes were cast off, and the initial gentle rolling movement of the vessel changed with a purpose as the harbour bar was cleared and they headed out through a tang of seaweed and salt into the open sea. The helpful breeze in the almost clear blue sky made cool work for the crew. After an increasingly chill night he wasn't all that distressed to be found the following morning as the cold and the first pangs of hunger made themselves felt. On being taken to face the Captain he was shaken, shouted at, questioned and made to feel considerably less than useless. Put to work in the galley in charge of an evil smelling but otherwise affable cook, he began to feel more at ease with his circumstances and formed the impression that this might all have happened once or twice before.

It very soon did so again. The voyage to Chatham was broken at Boston on the south Lincolnshire coast to take on more supplies and cargo, mostly grain. Within an hour or so they were under way again. He was lifting a bucket of water from over the side and watching the Boston stump fading into the dusk when he heard a commotion from one of the hatches, raised voices and cursing, and another voice more weary than surprised saying "It's another one". Almost immediately, a lad of about his own age was being propelled in the direction of the quarter deck emerging not long afterwards looking hot, uncomfortable and led by the left ear to be added to the cook's growing but vastly inexperienced culinary army.

His name turned out to be Jonathan North. Unlike Fenwick, he had come from a big family. Large enough for himself and later his younger sister Miriam to be farmed out with a childless couple, neighbours and friends of their parents, who had pleaded to help bring up the latest arrival. Well into middle age they nevertheless became excellent foster parents. Jonathan's foster-father had worked in that part of Lincolnshire for a number of years in the building of the new canals, eventually settling in Horncastle working the canal boats. Hence Jonathan's attachment to ships and shipping leading to a gradual urge to run away to sea.

The two lads, both about twelve, struck up a close friendship and resolved to stick together when they got to Chatham and to find a ship together. The ship's crew were very tolerant and cheery to the two, some of them perhaps recalling their own seafaring origins. Nevertheless, they got a further ticking off from the First-mate when they eventually docked at Chatham. Many of the crew gave them an encouraging wave, and with all the youthful optimism ever associated with their years, together with a cloth of bread and some cheese apiece, a few kindly donated and useful pence in their pockets, they set off towards whatever the future might have in store.

Unbeknown to them, word of mouth months later, in Jonathan's case many months later, reached their homes and confirmed their families' anguished suppositions and eventual hopes, thereby putting slightly to one side the aching, anguished, parental fear of the totally unknown.

Conversations with members of the crew on the voyage south had led them to a friendly Press Gang officer who would be prepared to help them sign up with a command of their own choosing, provided only that they signed up through him.

"I suppose from up north you'll be wanting to sail under Collingwood?"

They looked at each other and nodded, Jonathan not recalling being called a northerner before.

"Well, you'll get fair treatment in his navy, I'll say that, but don't ever step out of line or you'll be for it. He's strict on discipline and sees that's the fashion in all of his ships. Nelson leaves his Captains a freer hand so you might get fair treatment or you might get a real bastard. On the other hand, with Nelson there's more chance of death or glory, but there's no saying in what order." He paused, quietly amused, watching the boys' faces for reactions.

"Whichever you sail under there's certain to be battles with the French and Spanish, always, invasion or no invasion, and sometimes with the Americans. How about the '*Royal Sovereign*' here in Chatham almost fitted out? A very fine new ship of the line. Just about the biggest and fastest we've got. It's one of Collingwood's but won't be his flagship. So when the fighting starts you shouldn't be first into the thick of it. His style is to head his flagship straight into the enemy line, taking all they throw at him until he's right in among them in his chosen position, and then God help them from his broadsides. You'll find out all about them later I'll be bound."

So, Collingwood's '*Royal Sovereign*' got another two young volunteers reporting for duty. The immediate beneficiary of this mixed blessing was the Ship's Carpenter, it being Fenwick's suggestion to ask for that posting in the hope of avoiding more drudgery in the galley, or worse.

Life aboard was cramped and spartan but relatively clean and tidy compared with the other older and much smaller vessels they had known. Their training involved all manner of equipment maintenance aboard and they rapidly grew in confidence and ability once they had survived the initiation period which elders but not necessarily betters inflict on beginners in most walks of life.

When action stations sounded, their duties then became the support of the gun crews, fetching and carrying all types of supplies from the stores below to the gun decks. They filled every bucket, pail and tub with water. They struggled with arm-wrenching loads of powder, shot, and firing hemp, each gun crew demanding attention first. This was no mere rivalry although that had a lot to do with it. It was known that the largest of the enemy ships, in particular the huge Spanish warships, took some five minutes between their fearful broadsides, clearing, reloading, realigning, sighting and firing. Collingwood demanded of his crews three broadsides in that time and copious disciplined gun practices were dedicated to achieving it. The gun crews of his current flagship *'Dreadnought'* would claim to loose off three broadsides in three and a half minutes and many a dockside ale house brawl erupted when this was challenged by other brave but sceptical crews.

The effect of such close quarters broadsides in rapid succession was likely to be calamitous to the very structure of the enemy ships and the effect on the crew's morale devastating. Provided only that the opening enemy gunnery was not too accurate or damaging, our short-range gunfire from a crucial close-in position of advantage was confidently expected to turn the battle irrevocably in our favour. It usually did.

Later in the year the news came that Collingwood was transferring his flag to the '*Royal Sovereign*' stimulating much anticipation and a sliver of apprehension among the crew, not excepting our two shipmates. The next thing to happen was the disembarking of the Ship's Officers' wives in conjunction with sundry other womenfolk and, with the former, the general supervising care which many of them creditably assumed over the welfare of the younger members of the ship's crew. An atmosphere of battle preparedness began to pervade the big ship.

The reason for change soon became clear. Nelson had informed his Captains that the French and Spanish fleets had to be drawn into a fight following which our anticipated mastery of the Channel would finally persuade Napoleon that a successful invasion of our island would no longer be possible.

For years fears of an invasion from France had gripped the nation and the Royal Navy had made huge efforts blockading French and Spanish ports to prevent it. Ashore, the Government ordered that women, as well as children, were evacuated from all the possible invasion areas. Local impromptu volunteer militia were organised to resist the expected initial enemy landings. Shore defences and signalling systems were constructed in a climate of national fervour. Apprehensive but determined defiance pervaded the land. Across a very short stretch of water a continental dictator more inclined to fight a land war to his east cast a fretful eye in our direction and pondered his chances.

The nation identified and placed its faith in its one charismatic and easily recognisable leader,

Nelson, cheerfully vilifying the opinionated but clearly dangerous enemy caricature controlling the nearby continental landmass. Entertainers and commentators bolstered morale at home with popular songs extolling the heroism and leadership of the renowned Nelson, coupled with jokes in defiance of 'Old Boney' and the prospect of invasion; an unpredictable but easily imagined horror. The Armada and everything flung at the realm for the greater part of a millennium had so far failed. What chance Bonaparte?

After much diligent searching and skirmishing in both home and foreign waters, battle was decidedly joined late in October 1805 off Cape Trafalgar in heavy swells and a storm brewing. Superfluous stores, boxes and casks were thrown overboard. Stools, netting, hammocks and all movables were stored away and firmly secured. Gun crews made tense arrangements with their mates handing over personal effects with deeply felt but often hesitantly articulated messages for wives, mothers or kinfolk. Then, stripping to the waist and tying headbands over their ears in anticipation of the deafening roar of cannon-fire, they focussed to a man on their own gun and their own dedicated purpose. To Fenwick's and Jonathan's chagrin and not very well disguised apprehension, Collingwood made the fleet's first contact with the enemy, the '*Royal Sovereign*' splitting the enemy's orderly but not too well formed line ahead. After a seeming eternity enduring the enemy's opening broadsides while getting into position, Collingwood then let fly alternately to port and starboard with his main guns, and raking fore and aft as the opportunity presented with carronades. His flagship was soon surrounded and heavily pounded by no less than five tenacious French and Spanish warships, including the massive Spanish first rate '*Santa Ana*'.

Suffering alone in their concentrated fire especially from the stubborn French '*Fougueux*' for a further harrowing fifteen minutes, the '*Royal Sovereign*' then poured out her own ferocious broadsides. A devastating alternative as they slewed past the less well-protected rear structure of an enemy warship was to fire successive shots from each gun as it slowly swept by. At point blank range the first shots would shatter the timbers of the rear quarters, opening up the interior of the hull and the unprotected crew to the following devastating gunshots. The air was thick with gunpowder, shot, flame and clouds of smoke. So heavy and thick the ferocious crossfire, shot was even colliding with shot in mid air between opposing ships.

Almost the entire fleet was shortly engaged and the battle became a near chaos of burning, exploding, disintegrating and sinking or fleeing ships. Deafening noise and acrid smoke deadened the senses. The two boys had imagined nothing like it. If they had they probably would never have set sail with the navy. More water was fetched to swab away blood and entrails than was ever drunk or splashed on themselves by the crews. Curses, screams and orders rent the powder-charged air and in the flashing, flickering confusion wounded were carried or helped below and the dead turned slowly but purposefully overboard.

Fenwick had been called away during the final stages of the battle to help with the rigging of towlines. First of all to secure the vast Spanish flagship the

'*Santa Ana*' which had surrendered to Collingwood after receiving extensive structural damage. Then, as an untimely and perverse storm struck, enabling the '*Santa Ana*' to effect her escape, to secure their own seriously damaged but victorious warship to Captain Blackwood's frigate '*Euryalus*'. It was late on in the evening when Fenwick realised that he had not seen Jonathan for some time. Searching apprehensively he eventually found him in the makeshift and by this time grossly overcrowded ship's hospital. This was set up amidships on the lower deck along by the cockpit prepared for the Surgeon. A bad cut to the left side of Jonathan's head and shattered splintering timber some of which was clearly still embedded in his side left him blood saturated and near lifeless. Calling his name and carefully pouring some water into his open mouth, Fenwick found himself pushed to one side and a voice saying "Leave this to us, son."

He himself had been much luckier. Cuts to his legs and knees scrambling over smashed and jagged timbering, together with similarly caused cuts to his knuckles were all he had to complain about and to be thankful for. He thanked his Maker for his survival in one relatively undamaged piece and curled up exhausted for a few hours of well delayed but equally well needed sleep.

Chapter 3 - Clem and Rosina

Matt Robson ran homewards down the deeply rutted track, every jogging jarring step reminding him painfully of his own near calamity scarcely an hour or so earlier. His boots lashed through the Hare's-tail tufts of grass and the long narrow leaves already sturdily sprouting in and around the wagon wheel ruts. Not many weeks earlier these ruts had been ice solid and often during the year they were muddy linear pools waiting their chance to launch themselves at the unwary or unfortunate citizenry as jolting passing wheels provided a means of propulsion.

His mother Rosina met him at the gate. The imminent end of the world had evidently not been enough to deprive her of the presence of mind to put on her oldest and least favoured but handy shawl before joining her husband, Clem, in putting out the many fiery embers falling from the darkened sky on their fortunately slate tiled cottage and on its surrounds. The yellow jasmine scrambling up the stone walls was already copiously flecked with black dust. As a concession to the burning aerial missiles she had at least rolled down her knitted woollen sleeves. Even in the depths of winter and in the face of the most malevolent north easterlies of Siberian origin her bare arms would be hanging up the washing on a wavering outside line. In that sturdy resilience she was by no means alone in the sisterhood of the locality.

"Where's dad?"

"He's just this minute gone up to the cottages next the Hall to see if those old folk are all right. He'll check on the old widow woman that Fenwick stayed with when he first came here and perhaps see Katherine." Matt's sister was in service up at Felling Hall. Service was almost a family tradition as her mother and grandmother had many years between them serving in various capacities at both Felling and Gateshead Halls among other places. Well thought of, diligent and reliable, word of mouth among the gentlewomen of the area's wealthier families usually found them steady albeit lowly paid work.

The darkened skies had thoroughly confused the birds. The noise and the flying debris were disorientating enough without being followed by an untimely nightfall. Only an eclipse of the sun itself could have confused them more. They swooped and twittered in baffled incomprehension. Dogs slunk about in nervous wary wide-eyed anxiety and cats were nowhere to be seen.

John Hodgson, the young but already highly appreciated pastor of the nearby old Heworth Chapel was among the first to arrive at the centre of the disaster. The noise and very visible calamity soon brought quarrymen, shipyard workers, potters and all manners of tradesmen and labourers hustling to the pithead. The underground tremor had been felt in collieries for miles around, as far as Sunderland, and local colliers arrived in droves to help the rescue efforts. The Reverend Hodgson, as he was universally known, became a focus for the devastated community and soon shouldered the dual load of his ministry to the victim's families and also to their future care for which he already knew there would be scant provision. Among the first of many melancholy duties that afternoon for him was to say the last rites over three young boys, their under-sized bodies far too badly mutilated for them to survive their dreadful injuries.

A further explosion had scattered the crowd and caused more terror until it was realised it was some sort of after explosion, following on from the first ones and perversely beneficial in that it helped clear some of the dreaded after-damp from below. There was no shortage of volunteers, experienced underground or not, including toll-keeper Joe from the nearby new turnpike road, joining in the briefly interrupted recovery work.

Five rescuers were immediately brought up. Two were still left below. After their eventual return to safety, the overman and viewer decided to abandon any further rescue attempts until the underground fires were extinguished and the air in the workings became tolerable for breathing and seeing. The reaction of many in the crowd was an understandable frustrated anger and a wretched agonized resentment. It was unbearable that close relatives and friends still entombed underground were apparently being deserted and abandoned to a cold, dark and desolate fate.

John Hodgson worked late into the night comforting the distraught, counselling the frustrated and headstrong, taking such detail as he could of the injured and missing, and joining this group and that in prayer.

Clem and Rosina didn't get much sleep that night either. They did what they could to help until it was clear that no further rescue attempt would be made at least until daylight. The three youngest children had been put to bed including Thomas, all of thirteen years old and now a riverside stable lad. Clem had so far succeeded in keeping him out of the pit. This, he regarded as some success in comparison with his feeling of failure when his eldest, Matt, could not be dissuaded from following his father into the Felling colliery. At least he could keep his eye on him there, he thought, and watch out for opportunities of more skilled work on the surface, perhaps as an engineman or winder.

His own accident about two years ago had abruptly ended a fairly good run of well-paid years hewing much needed coal for the Napoleonic wars. A roof fall, a broken hip and fractured left leg, a hurried trip by cart to the Infirmary in Newcastle and several weeks of hospitalised recovery in the Keelmen's had rendered him useless to any future as a miner. He could turn his hand to most things however, repairing boots and shoes, even occasionally mending fellow miner's clocks. From the plot around the cottage he produced useful supplies of potatoes and vegetables. His family did not want.

The cottage had been unoccupied and becoming derelict for some time before he and Rosina married.

He jumped at an offer from the Brandling family, owners of the Hall and of the colliery, of a five-year lease at a modest rent on condition that he restored the cottage and also signed his yearly bond. The rebuilding he had done to a creditable standard, replacing the clay floor and adapting the small loft area under the roof timbers to bedding space for the children as they grew from babyhood. They had five, not counting two miscarriages. Not counted by others, that is.

The Brandlings were a very long established and wealthy local family. Their associations with The Felling and Felling Hall went back at least to Elizabethan years. At times unpredictable and often disconcertingly blunt, they were best not to be crossed. But that was true of many, in elevated places or not. Clem and Rosina never knew if the offer of the cottage was a kindness in recognition of her years of service in their households, a means of holding on to the industrious Clem, or a bit of both. Better-placed observers might have included it in the general tidying up and gradual selling off of family possessions as the Brandling clan transferred their epicentre a few miles northwards to rural Gosforth Park.

After his accident, Clem applied himself to making and repairing corves, tough wicker baskets of various sizes used by the miners to move coal and to load it onto the underground trams and wagons. This hard but dextrous work he could carry out from home. Most of the time seated, he was able to minimise his painful and ungainly efforts at walking.

Those had been the hard years. It had certainly helped that Matt was now earning, a few shillings were coming in from Katherine's service at the old Hall and also from Thomas at the stables down Felling Shore. Clem had been putting by purchases of stone and tiles intending to add an extension to the cottage and had to shelve his plans when his accident struck. The unexpected arrival of his wife's young cousin Fenwick revived those plans. The extensions were then completed with the help of Fenwick's labour and not a few guineas from his savings. The extra room now housed Fenwick and the two boys. The two youngest girls delighted in being moved up into the loft space now vacated by their brothers. Their greatest excitement was sharing their space with Katherine, who lived in at the Hall but occasionally stayed at home overnight. Mother and eldest sister had their work cut out those nights to get them settled down and sleeping.

Rosina was an attractive and hardworking woman, black hair prematurely greying. A largish family and the hard work that went with it never fazed her. She had always assumed and hoped that she would marry someone like Clem and raise a family of her own. Her experience of working in the homes of the wealthy had not led to envy or resentment of her own evident lower circumstances. The people in positions of authority and comfort she could clearly see had their own shortcomings and Rosina viewed positions in life as no more than chances of fate. That was the way the world was and there was little to be done about it. She was content, with one proviso. Year on year the world had to be getting better. She had to have the sustaining optimism that her generation and her children would have somewhat better and less arduous lives than her parents and grandparents ever had. Her diligence and Clem's hard work had to result in that. The yardstick and hopes of many people the world over.

Only a very small minority of the local working women could read or write. Perhaps only half of the men could. As a child, Rosina remembered her mother telling the tale of how she 'made her mark` signing her wedding lines. She resolved when her turn came she would be able to sign her name like an educated person. With Clem's help she learned to do that with painstaking pride and further resolved that whatever children she might have, boys and girls, they would all learn to read and write. To her credit they all did.

The following morning a huge crowd was gathering at the pithead. Vociferous and impatient miners, in particular from Sunderland and the length of the lower Wear valley, were calling for action. Volunteers for rescue parties abounded. The overmen and viewer insisted that nothing could be achieved until the fire underground was out and that meant closing off the air supply. Almost everyone recognised the brutally harrowing but starkly lethal logic. Everyone was agitated with the imposed inaction.

Accusations of cowardice and bribery were flung about by very heated and very raised voices. Equally angry and resentful voices defended the colliery overmen and local managers. The coal owners insisted no money would be spared to help the rescue and recovery efforts once the mine was safe to re-enter. The Constables were hard put to keep order. The calm voice of John Hodgson summed up the painful truth. There had been fatalities. Almost certainly more would be discovered and confirmed. The bereaved families needed immediate care and would need long-term support. Among other things he had arranged a public meeting at the 'Wheatsheaf' that evening to open a disaster fund and organise its management. Already, he had provoked the anger of many coal owners by assisting local newspapermen to publish the disaster in great detail. This was very much against the long running cosy custom and self-protective practice of the owners not to have their mining fatalities published by the press.

- o 0 o -

"He's a varry clivvor man, the Reverend Hodgson," observed young Thomas. "A very clever man" agreed his mother. Rosina instinctively corrected the broader dialect as she went along. It was by now second nature, part of her accepted role in life. One of the ways she could see to 'raise the standards', although she would probably admit to more success in this regard with the female members of her brood than the other wayward lot. She carried on clearing the table.

"Down at the yard they say he's always at war with the coal owners."

"Be careful what you repeat, son" said Clem. "You never know who might take offence, and one day it might cost you your job. I've heard that the Reverend Hodgson doesn't get along with the coal owners because they all got together and agreed not to have details of accidents in their mines mentioned in the papers."

"It seems to me, Clem, they keep tight hold of their money and give nowt to widows and families and the like," added Fenwick.

"Well, that's as may be, but I have to speak as I find, and the Brandlings did all right by me when I had my accident. Where's Matt?"

"He slipped away as soon as he'd finished eating. His shoulder's still very sore. Probably hoping to see that little fair-haired Methodist girl he got to know at the classes."

"Methodist?" Clem paused; to be sure Rosina was still listening. "Could be worse."

Rosina knew without looking round that she was expected to rise to the bait. In their early years together she had fallen for it so many times. Now, it was a subtle mutual game. She wouldn't concede eye contact or even curiosity. Curiosity least of all. Nevertheless, "What worse?"

"Could have been a papist." Clem raised an eyebrow and half closed the balancing eye, watching for her reaction. She made none, apart from an almost imperceptible and dismissive sniff. They both smiled to themselves. Another draw.

"Down the mine's like being on board ship," volunteered Fenwick. You're all in it together, church, chapel or whatever and you get along. Especially when the action starts. On some Navy ships half the crew are Irishers and Catholics. Cannonshot doesn't see the difference." That about summed up attitudes. A long history of imposed supremacies, founded less in faith than finance, had produced a local culture of toleration.

This would long be a creditable characteristic in the area, though doubtless not unique in the kingdom.

Rosina cleared up after the meal, putting away the crockery in the glass-fronted shelved dresser taking pride of place, centre-wall, facing the front door and intentionally unmissable by every visitor. It was, in fact, two pieces of furniture. The lower part was a four-drawer oak chest given to Rosina as a wedding present and the upper portion, of similar wood and general design later acquired at a Felling Hall sale, neatly combined into quite an imposing dresser by a Felling Shore cabinetmaker. The proverbial man on a galloping horse would not have guessed at their earlier separate identities. She had a few pieces of decent china and glassware on view and imagined the day when there might be much more. Perhaps they would grace a proper house along with one of the new Broadwood pianos in the drawing room and the girls sitting in their elegant finest, playing duets on the glistening keys.

Putting on a better shawl than earlier, a couple of deft swipes at her skirt and a final check for recalcitrant strands of hair, she set off for the pithead carrying a basket of bread and cheese plus a few cooked sausages for the disconsolate souls unable or unwilling to leave the disaster scene. Her menfolk followed with blankets. From many a modest home and cottage came similar provisions and offers of a roof for the night. It would be a very long night, so it would, and so would be very many more.

**Chapter 4 - After the Battle**

In the fading natural light augmented by the glow of burning hulks, and in the face of the gathering storm, all hands now laboured to save the still living from the unremitting sea. The battle won and lost, the cannon, the carronades and the muskets now silent, enemies but an hour or so since joined endeavours to haul the injured, the exhausted and the desperate from the debris littered blackened and bloodied seas.

The surviving British fleet and its captured remnant prizes rode out the storm and headed for the safety and succour of Gibraltar. Fenwick was much relieved that Jonathan pulled through and very gradually recovered his strength. Jonathan was the taller of the two but thin. Fenwick was a mite shorter than average and would always look smaller than he actually was, because of tapering shoulders that happened to conceal quite a deep chest. These deceptive physical elements of strength and endurance combined later in life with unintentionally deceptive elements in his personal presentation to add some mystery and unconventionality to his character.

The journey to Gib. was a busy one. The '*Royal Sovereign*' had herself taken quite a battering and temporary repair work was followed by such permanent restitution as could be managed with the materials to hand. Fenwick visited Jonathan every day possible and helped him back on his feet. The day after the battle a tattered and bloodied French prisoner had been lowered onto the hospital floor alongside Jonathan. To be more precise, this was a scrap of near drowned humanity given perhaps less chance of survival than Jonathan, a French sailor boy even younger than our two, much smaller and skinnier than either. Not the size of a decent scrubbing brush, Rosina might have said. The two badly injured boys may have been placed together for convenience of medical attention or for some mutual reassurance in a frightening world. However, survive they both did.

The lower gun deck had been cleared as much as possible and turned into use for the holding of French and Spanish prisoners under the supervision of the Marines.

"Let's go down and see if we can find that little French lad," Jonathan suggested after a week or so, having recovered well enough to get about the ship. "They took him out to put him among the other Frenchies. He's only but a nipper. I've asked around and *nom* means name. *Ami* is friend and none of the gunners seem to know anything else useful." He and Fenwick set off below and persuaded the attending Marines to let them locate and visit the diminutive and unsuspecting French captive.

They found him sitting on the gun deck, propped up against the back wheel of a gun carriage looking pale and frail, almost lost in the ludicrously oversized clothes hastily found for him. He grinned a welcoming smile of recognition and made to get up but his visitors sat down cross-legged beside him. The opening jumble of *bon jour* and *hullos* soon collapsed into friendly frustrated laughter all round with English hands and arms waving about in hopeful descriptive support just as much as French ones. Jonathan fortunately remembered his extensive homework and directed his two words of French in the appropriate direction.

"Je m'appelle Benoit Halle. Benoit Halle," came the reply.

"But that's a Newcastle name" exclaimed an amazed Fenwick. "I have an aunt who worked at Benwell Hall. "That really does take the biscuit that does!"

It took many visits of mystification and hilarity to achieve a useful level of understanding and even then the grasp was never ever nearly complete. The respective dialects were a major initial hazard until ears tuned in to increasingly recognisable words. Benoit did recognise *Newcastle,* with good reason, but first off he thought *an aunt* was a reference to his own hometown, Nantes in Brittany.

Over many visits, and with surprisingly extensive vocabulary gleaned from a variety of mutual shipmates the three were able to convey a quite a lot to each other. Benoit had been allowed to leave home in the custody and company of two of his uncles. All had signed up for the '*Fougueux*', all were fished out of the sea clinging to a tangle of spars and decking, all had been injured,

Benoit and one of his uncles quite badly. The badly injured uncle was still in the ship's hospital, recovering but still too weak to be moved. This poor fellow since birth had always been several centimes short of the full franc or however the French might choose to put it. His older brother was always with him and cared for him as protectively as any mother hen. So, even as young as he was, Benoit was scarcely an extra burden.

Benoit was able to relate in graphic detail the tales he had been told of the revolutionary events in Nantes. The available guillotines were so overworked; the tribunal authorities resorted without compunction to tying up condemned prisoners and tipping them from barges to drown desperately and futilely struggling for their lives in the River Loire. "Incroyable". Before joining the '*Fougueux*' he and his uncles had spent some two years working supply ships building up one of Napoleon's three great armies preparing for the long awaited invasion of England. The army they had been assisting was the one based on Dunkirk, with orders to assault the North East Coast and take Newcastle. That name therefore rang quite an accurate bell. Shiploads of soldiers who had embarked for the invasion and then forced to return to shore had mutinied. Minds higher up were neither focussed nor confident. Lives lower down were of little worth.

Until they docked in Gibraltar where they lost touch with him they plied Benoit with whatever additional food they could obtain from the galley and from their own mess. There was usually extra bread, ham, cheese and beer to be had. After all the prisoners had been disembarked they couldn't find where he might have gone. The best they could glean from the Marines was that he was likely to fetch up in Chatham in one of the hulks used for prisoners before being moved to an on-shore prisoner of war camp. That was encouraging as they, more than likely, would be ordered back to Chatham for further repair and refitting.

Chatham it was. Some of the ships were laid up for repair and refitting and a large number of sailors were paid off. Almost their own final naval duty before discharge was to support their much embraided superiors attending the magnificent state funeral of their hero Lord Nelson in the City of London. This was for them both a first glimpse of the capital leading to a shared interest in making further visits of exploration.

In the general demobilisation of the navy after Trafalgar they both managed to get jobs in Chatham's huge sprawling naval facility. On many an early morning they scampered breathless and still half asleep, from their nearby lodgings hurrying through the dockyard gates urged on by the intensifying toll of the warning bell as the gates closed inexorably on tardy stragglers. No work that day for those unfortunates.

Early on, they managed to locate Benoit in one of the grim prison hulks down river. His badly injured uncle, unfortunately, had not survived. With his other uncle, he was waiting to be transported to hopefully better conditions in a prisoner of war camp at Norman Cross, somewhere near rural Peterborough. From there they hoped to be returned to France either through general peace terms or through a periodically agreed exchange of prisoners.

The dockyard at Chatham was almost a city in itself, a veritable hive of activities. All forms of large-scale construction and repair were going on. Timber, metal and rope as far as the eye could see. The rope works itself was more than a quarter of a mile in length, housing an ingenious machine winding ropes and hawsers as thick as tree trunks and as long as needed. Nearby, to their wary delight, worked scores of dextrous and lively girls occupied in the generation of every conceivable finer rope or twine known to nautical man.

The two boys, along with every other young blade in the yard, dreaded being sent on some works errand to the female supervisors of these girls. These formidable custodians were always to be found at the far end of their workshops for reasons of vantage. This left every young male visitor making his way along the central gangway beware the hazard of skirted legs flicking out to trip him up, the rowdy female congregation boisterously revelling in anticipation of his embarrassment and confusion, and in their own comforting safety in numbers. It took a brave man to ignore the traps and an unwise one to react. Out in the town these girls prudently took good care to conceal from boyfriends as long as possible their workplace in Chatham, such was their notoriety.

They had some very good times, learned a lot both of work and of life, and thrived on the hard work. Then disaster struck. Jonathan had never really recovered from his serious wounds at Trafalgar. In the words of one older gunner at the time, "He'll carry those marks to his grave!" One winter he contracted pneumonia. In the hospital bay he feared the worst and asked Fenwick for his help. He wanted his few possessions and his bounty money to be given to his sister, Miriam. His premonitions were well founded and two days later a distraught Fenwick had lost his friend.

He had attended many funerals, afloat and on land, but this affected him deeply and to the core. The two had become as brothers, Fenwick doubtless the more isolated than if the positions had been reversed. The pristine new chapel at the Chatham dockyard, holding one of the very first of such services, was itself a poignant reminder of happier days. They had laboured together for many weeks in its fitting out. The taller, thinner, Jonathan had been a willing accomplice in many an escapade. Rarely the initiator, he was never a complainer when things went wrong.

Not previously having thought too much about the future, Fenwick now felt he had to come to some decisions. Should he remain at Chatham and wait for whatever the future might bring? Move on somewhere else? Should he return north and see his parents? Perhaps they would understand and forgive him. Perhaps they would not.

He was young. He had no responsibilities other than his firm promise to Jonathan and he was confident in finding work wherever he pitched up. The hollow feeling in his stomach wasn't likely to leave him while memories struck him at every turn in Chatham. He would take the opportunity to see something of England other than just some of its ports. He would travel overland to Lincolnshire to fulfil his obligation. Peterborough and possibly Benoit were on the way. Afterwards, he would continue north through Lincoln,

York and Durham, seeing their great cathedrals. An old interest had been rekindled on seeing Wren's fabulous new St. Paul's in the City of London at Nelson's impressive state funeral.

The journey north was an adventure in itself. Whenever possible, he rode on the top of the coach rather than inside where the relative comfort cost so much more. On occasion he would be up front alongside the driver or on a rear-facing seat at the back. The combination of his youth and his naval service stood him in good stead with the coachmen. Helping out with passengers, hefting their luggage and freight earned him not a few hot meals and coin of the realm. The hot meals in the company of the coachmen were particularly welcome, as he had not fully appreciated the deadening cold of outside passenger travel at night and in the early mornings. Wearing as much of his available clothing as he could, coupled with the incessant jolting of the primitively sprung coaches on the even more primitively tended roads, his circulation managed to sustain his aching and uncomfortable survival.

The coachmen were full of tales of experiences with highwaymen but, slightly to Fenwick's disappointment and rather more to his private relief, nothing of that nature happened on his journey to Peterborough or afterwards. Perhaps, he thought, he never travelled on stagecoaches looking at all likely to be carrying enough wealth to attract serious thieves.

At Peterborough he found a wagon taking fresh food supplies to the Norman Cross prisoner of war camp. At first, the military guards were inclined to turn him away but they relented as he told his story and his reasons for turning up there. The mention of Trafalgar doubtless did the trick and he was shortly led along avenues of huts in a hopefully promising direction. He very soon spotted Benoit who had grown a bit and also filled out a bit, but was instantly recognisable. Fenwick had been given the best part of two hours by the guards but was instructed he must leave well before roll call.

They swapped experiences of the intervening years and commiserated on the losses they had both suffered, Jonathan in Fenwick's case and in Benoit's his unfortunate younger uncle, both true casualties of the defining and prodigious naval battle in which they had served on opposite sides. The older uncle had reluctantly been returned recently to their homeland in a prisoner exchange, mollified only partly by the prevailing expectancy that Benoit would soon be similarly repatriated. This had proved to be the case, and Benoit was expecting to return to France in a few weeks time.

Fenwick gave his friend some money to help him on his way and also handed him a small but attractive gift figurine in blue, white and yellow of a Vauxhall Gardens flower seller. He found himself being pressed in turn to accept the gift of a cleverly crafted and beautifully carved set of concentric rings for the securing of a lady's shawl or headscarf. These had been ingeniously worked from a shark's backbone during many a slow hour of imprisonment. In fact, the camp inmates turned their hands to all manner of ship's models, in or out of bottles, woodcarvings, toys, trinkets and curios from whatever materials they could get. These activities helped to while away the time and clandestine commercial arrangements with their guards by cash exchange or bartering served to make a modest but cherished improvement in their tedious circumstances.

The two unexpected shipmates parted in high spirits, the smiles and banter nevertheless masking the sharp awareness that they would probably never meet again.

- o 0 o -

The coach rattled into Horncastle and pulled heavily into the busy yard of the Black Bull. Chickens scattered noisily and even more noisily the dogs, which had followed the coach from the outskirts of this small but always busy town, barked and snapped and spoiled with the pack of waiting dogs proprietarily guarding their territorial yard. Fenwick got down and stretched his protesting bones. Hoisting his pack onto his shoulder he went into the Inn and got himself a small room for a few days. He was glad to have his feet on solid ground again with the prospect of some rest. Coaches were worse than ships by far. No room to move for hours on end and never ever as restful as a ship in a calm sea.

The sun was out and the little market town was lively and purposeful. Sad though his immediate duty was, he was already looking forward to his stay as he set off down the Boston Road to look for the home of the Appleby's, Jonathan and Miriam's foster parents. He recalled Jonathan's directions were this way out of town, somewhere between The Wong and Hangman's Corner. Checking his imaginary compass bearings with a couple of curious locals, he knocked on the door of the neat cottage that had been indicated.

Miriam came to the door. Turned sixteen, she had the complexion which might have been expected of a well cared for country girl, dark brown hair, fair skin with just a few freckles around her nose and an interested expression seemingly ready to break into a smile. The puppy fat might or might not go but she was already a credit to the care of the Appleby's.

"Miriam?"

The girl nodded and looked puzzled.

"I'm Fenwick Skipsey, a friend of …." Before he could get any more words out of his mouth she cried out "Jonathan's friend" and then paused searching his face for some other expression. In the same instant that she knew something was amiss, he knew sickeningly what he had feared for some time, she had not heard of Jonathan's death.

"What is it?" came a voice from inside and in the next step, Mrs. Appleby appeared, drying her hands and trying to understand the strangeness in the small scene in front of her.

Miriam turned. "Jonathan" was all she could get out before her contorted face and floods of physically uncontrollable tears told Betty Appleby all she needed to know. Pulling the girl to her, she guided her into the cottage beckoning Fenwick to follow as her own tears took over. The two women clung to each other a long time before Betty wiped her eyes and insisted Fenwick sat down. Betty had grieved hard and long when Jonathan first went missing. Today's news was final but not the first time she had felt being bereaved.

Miriam had missed her brother grievously when he ran off but she had not been altogether surprised at his departure. Young talk of going to sea had always seemed a pipe dream, at least until it happened.

She had been surprised and delighted to get a letter from him six months or so after Trafalgar. He had spoken of coming back to see her one day and she treasured the prospect. He had also mentioned having collected some injury. The lack of detail, as is usually the case with the female of the species, left her imagination its full apprehensive range. Nonetheless, she had not in her bones envisaged this outcome and was truly devastated.

After a while they plied him with questions until Betty Appleby effectively called a halt, apologising for the discomfort she said they must be causing Fenwick and made him promise to return the following day for a meal with them, to tell them of the happy times she was sure he and Jonathan had spent together.

Over several days Fenwick got to know Bill and Betty Appleby. Bill was a stableman and helped to manage a large stable off the Boston Road holding horses both for farm and domestic duties. Betty had been in domestic service, mainly in kitchens. For the most part a placid and contented couple, they had counted themselves unexpectedly blessed when, after too many childless years, they approached the Norths and were allowed to foster, first Jonathan then Miriam.

Miriam had been the livelier of the two children. The Applebys doted on her, encouraging and developing her every interest. She could easily have been spoilt, but wasn't. In fact she was popular in the neighbourhood, especially with the womenfolk. Her particular interest was in the making of jams, chutneys and cordials, pickling and preserving quite a variety and mixture of the copious fruits and berries freely available in the Lincolnshire countryside at various times of the year. She would be forever cajoling recipes for everything from elderberries to turnips and Betty's small kitchen would be a turmoil. Tomato jam and parsnip wine were favourites. The results were usually good, it has to be said, and as the basic ingredients inevitably came in seasonal gluts the frequent beneficiaries were the elderly poor in the almshouse up the road. There she had a number of devotees and from them learned much of local lore and hearsay. A happy trade for the occasional and not that infrequent tasty supplements to their worthy but basic parish fare.

Fenwick was certainly taken with this girl. The relationship and circumstances were, at the one and same time, inhibiting and attracting. Were his feelings for her partly familial because of his strong friendship with her brother? He felt uncomfortable with the thought that he could be taking advantage of his special position.

Betty saw some attraction between the two, but only of two young people enjoying each other's company and certainly no reason to fly any warning flags. After the evening meal with Bill she would insist on the teenage two turning out for a walk while she cleared away.

The evening before Fenwick was to continue his journey north, he and Miriam were returning to the cottage in the gathering dusk a little later than usual. It may have been because it was the last evening together.

Fenwick was never ever much good at stopping to analyse, but on impulse he kissed her. Truth be told, it was because it was their last evening together, and it was not an impulse.

They had been talking about nothing in particular, when he took her arm, drew her to him and quickly kissed her. She didn't seem surprised. Nor did she look all that taken aback or offended. Her young lips were soft and her eyes, which only closed briefly, then seemed to fix on his face with an expression part smile, part amusement? So he took a better grip on her upper arms, looked hard at her lips and kissed her firmly again, holding her close for some time without either of them speaking.

She had been wondering, half hoping, that he might be inclined to kiss her. This strangely spoken northerner was certainly interesting and quite attractive in a way. Hence her smile, not of amusement, rather of a confirmed satisfaction of her interest to him. They looked at each other, half smiling. He thought to continue; she hesitated for a moment and was unable to restrain an unwanted and embarrassed little girlish giggle.

On either of them decision or initiative was saved. The sound of imminently approaching footsteps came through the nearby brushwood. They drew apart.

Frank Whitely was well known to Miriam and, for that matter, to everyone else hereabouts. His loose dark brown coat, especially in the evenings, was often known to hold a rabbit or perhaps two. Most of the local gamekeepers had him down as a marked man and bided their time. Whitely was confident in his ability to keep at least one step ahead and affected an affable but none the less disparaging relationship with all of them.

He was perhaps three years or so older than Miriam. In the past year or more he had shown an increasing interest in her, usually at the local social events centred on the township's parish church, St. Mary's. She had felt just a bit flattered that a confident young fellow, older than most of the boys she had known so well since childhood, had singled her out. Pleased also that his interest was noted, and remarked on, by the other girls.

"Oh. Hello, Miriam."

"Hello."

Frank Whitely took in the scene, especially Fenwick. He was alert to the situation in a way Fenwick was not. Always aware of the main chance, he supplemented his income from his father's farm with whatever else might present itself, skirting the law too closely at times. A childhood brush with smallpox had left him with some slight pockmarks to the face. To him this became the cause of some self-consciousness, later compensated by an assertiveness beyond his years. His face was all the more manly, and his manner all the more attractive to the local girls, than he was to realise for some time.

Under stress, he often made anarchic hand movements as if overstressing an unimportant point. Those who knew him well were no longer consciously aware of the characteristic. Nor was he. Strangers however, would note this and make no comment, at least in his presence. Perhaps this was not a fellow to fall out with.

He knew who Fenwick was, of course. He scarcely paused as he walked past them and was soon out of view.

"We'd better be getting back." The spell of the moment broken, they returned to the cottage where Fenwick said his goodbyes with strangely mixed feelings. Neither he nor Miriam felt that they had met the love of their lives but a bond and an attraction were certainly there. Had they been a little older they both had the notion that their brief friendship might perhaps have developed into something closer.

As the early morning coach rumbled north to Lincoln the following day, Fenwick had plenty to occupy his thoughts and the jolting of the ride was in harmony with his feelings. A deeply sensitive soul he was not, and time would tell if his present turmoil was a passing sensation or not.

- o 0 o -

Late the afternoon the day after, Miriam was engrossed with her thoughts and the gathering of berries from some hedgerows a little distance from home. She felt she needed time to herself to reflect in solitude and this was an ideal occupation in the warm dry weather. For some reason she sensed that she was not alone and turned to see Frank Whitely not far away. He must have been watching her for quite a while and walked towards her when he realised she had become aware of his presence.

"Hello."

She guardedly returned his cool greeting and instinctively wiped her hands on her apron.

"I heard that your northern boyfriend has gone."

"He's not my boyfriend. He's a friend of Jonathan's from the Navy."

She moved to one side uncomfortably. This was not to be a friendly conversation. His hands were lifting and jerking as he spoke. There was a tense tone to his voice which she recalled hearing in the past, never addressed to her but to others perhaps in the market square as he explained some questioned activity. His eyes were wide, unsmiling, and accusing.

"I thought you ... I thought we ....were friends." His meaning was much clearer than the words coming out. Strained as he was, he knew he'd never declared an attraction to the girl fearing rejection and settling so far for friendly recognition and her smiling acceptance of his attention on those occasions when their paths happened to cross.

"Of course we're friends. Not special friends, but ...," her voice trembled and faltered. She strove despairingly for words and a womanly wisdom a little beyond her years to cope with this disturbing and unexpected developing situation. Like women throughout the ages, she instinctively began to accuse herself of giving him unintentional encouragement thinking of the vicarious pleasure she had taken when she had been sought out among her friends for some minor compliment or pleasantry.

He turned away and turned back.

"If he hadn't come here ...." His voice rose to a shout in a rage of incoherence and blind frustration. His hands went for her throat and gripped with a passion he had never known. She gripped and then tore at his hands and tried to scream through the unbearable pain. The crazed unrecognisable creature in front of her was in a fury beyond belief and certainly beyond any sort of compassion. She struggled desperately for breath in her ever-increasing terror and her ebbing inadequate strength. The world was turning red, spinning, lights were quivering, her strength was going, and then it was over.

Her body gave way under his grip. He staggered forward under its weight and let go. Intuitively, he knew that she was dead. He very well recognised sudden death following spirited life. The appalling horror of what he had done struck immediately and he was transfixed with a numb incredulity and a dawning terror. Pulling her body off the pathway and into a gap in the hedgerow his one thought was to get away, anywhere. With luck, Miriam would not be seriously missed until after dark. A horse and saddle should be easy. He had been to Nottingham once in the past but wouldn't be known or recognised there. A big place. Nottingham then.

Chapter 5 - Killingworth and George Stephenson

The Sunday after the disaster a packed Heworth Chapel listened to the consoling words of John Hodgson. His large, expectedly large, assembly sat attentively in a still stunned stoic silence. Searching the essence of his ministry, this dedicated man found words to help the grief so clear in so many of the bewildered and familiar faces in front of him. Well aware that his words would help some less than others in their personal distress, he sought to lift spirits generally and focus on a common resolve which could help to sustain all of those suffering the agonies of sudden loss. He knew that the despondency would eventually lift and it would lift all the sooner if his community bonded to deal with this stark and indiscriminate calamity.

After the service he stood at the door with words of consolation for many, and words of pending action for many others. He was determined to encourage and, if need be, lead an appeal for significant funds to care for the victims and their families on an established basis well into the future. Attitudes from the past, whereby the coal owners in particular took little or no responsibility for their employees' welfare following injuries or even fatalities, could no longer be endured. His own position of appointment might well come into question. If so, he would have to make his case and stand by it.

"The meeting on Wednesday at the Wheatsheaf set up a disaster fund and all week I've had people pressing me to take money from them to help the suffering families. Some with immediate needs I've been able to help already. Ship's crews have passed the hat round, you'll have seen the street collections and I've been told some collieries are giving a day's pay. The newspapers are opening subscription lists and I'm very hopeful we'll get somewhere. Out of such a tragedy it's wonderful to see such generosity. His Grace the Bishop of Durham made the first donation and it was matched here by Mr. Charles Brandling."

"We won't be here the Sunday after next," said Clem as he shook hands at the gate. "We're arranging to go to Rosina's sister's at Killingworth to see if there's any work going for Matt and Fenwick. If the Felling pits ever open again it's going to be a long, long time before they do."

"But you and Rosina and the younger children won't be leaving The Felling?"

"We don't expect so. At least for the time being."

"I've had a word with Tommy's boss. He has a horse and dray we can share for our trip to Killingworth Sunday coming."

"Share?" Rosina wasn't sure she liked the sound of that.

"We're lucky to get anything at all," explained Clem. "Sound horses are in short supply but they have a regular arrangement with those two catholic sisters at Heworth to take them to the RC church, St. Andrews, top of Pilgrim Street, Newcastle. Locals and others come from miles around. They will spend the day with friends while we go on to Killingworth, picking them up on the way back."

"The older one's quite canny, but the younger one's always up a height," reflected Rosina.

Ignoring the objection on the grounds that anything he said would be considered inadequate by her and irrelevant anyway by himself, he pressed on. "Once we're over the Tyne Bridge the grown-ups will need to get down and walk. The steep slope of Pilgrim Street would be too much for the horse to pull us all. Same coming back up Bottle Bank in Gateshead."

For the younger children the journey to Killingworth was the event of a lifetime. Sitting on sacks of hay, listening to the grown-ups chatter and watching the world pass by. Their elders were only slightly less uncomfortable. Removable wooden benches each side of the dray were secured by posts upon which a tarpaulin could be spread in the event of rain. Well-worn and well-flattened leather cushioning covered the length of the benches to which modicum of comfort the ladies added some folds of the blankets they were advised to bring with them.

"Is this your regular Sunday morning?" politely enquired Rosina of the two sisters.

"Yes," replied the younger one. "Hail, rain or shine. The summer's better than the winter, though. I understand you're visiting relatives?"

"That's right. I have a brother-in-law at Killingworth who works with George Stephenson. Known the family for years. Since before his father's accident. Clem thinks there may be a chance of work going there for Matt and Fenwick. It'll be a long time they say, if ever, before the Felling pits can be reopened."

"We keep hearing of Mr. Stephenson. Must be a clever man", said the older one. "We met your Reverend Hodgson during the week. Lovely man. Always speaks. He was saying it's possible Mr. Stephenson might be coming to The Felling. Something about a safe lamp for the colliers. He also said they were planning to have a mass funeral for the victims from the John Pit rather than individual ones."

"Yes. He said that last week at our old chapel. It's all still too hard to credit, isn't it?"

- o 0 o -

"If your dinner's gone down enough, let's go along and see George Stephenson. He said he'd be at the colliery or thereabouts. It's not far. He's always up there on a Sunday afternoon. Always occupied. Always thinking about something. Always."

The men folk escaped the clearing away and the seamless domestic chatter. Sure enough, there was George Stephenson with sleeves rolled up, crouched half-kneeling on the boiler house floor. He was holding one end of a length of twine by a mark to one side of a large piece of steel plate.

"Come in, and welcome. I'll be with ye in half a moment." His rich Northumbrian brogue came with as broad a smile. "Hold this, son. Put your thumb tight there." He motioned to Matt to hold the end of the twine on a fine chalk mark while he straightened up and walked round to the other side of the plate, rubbing white chalk on the twine as he went. Carefully holding his end of the twine to another mark with his right thumb, he reached back as far as he could stretch across the metal plate. "Tight now." Picking up the taught twine in his left index finger and thumb, and a final glance in Matt's direction, he lifted the twine an inch or so upwards and let it go. The twine smacked back against the metal plate leaving a sharp, clear, straight, white line of chalk deposit between the two marks. "That'll be enough for the day, Bob," he indicated to one of the workmen nearby. "We'll cut that th' morra."

"Hello Tom, Clem. Matt, you've grown a bit." He shook hands all round. "And you must be Fenwick, Rosina's cousin I've heard tell of. Let's sit outside in the sun, we get little enough of it."

For best part of two hours the conversation ranged over every current topic and a few more besides. A tall, well-made man, George Stephenson could have been taken for a capable but modest farmer and clearly of no formal education. That reasonable first impression would soon give way to a deeper re-assessment. He listened more than he talked and seemed easily to absorb information on subjects that interested him. Of those there were many. His questions sought the far end of everything.

Not having met Fenwick before, he was soon engrossed in all the eager Fenwick could tell him of his time at Chatham. The unique rope-making machine and the Admiralty's signalling system down to Portsmouth he found fascinating. Fenwick wished he had more to relate about Mr. Brunel and his steam boiler at Chatham but to be honest, he had never been involved and, for once, felt this might be the wrong time to exaggerate.

He was relieved he hadn't when he realised that not only was George well aware of the public interest in London when 'Catch me as catch can' was steaming circles at Euston, but he and his father knew Richard Trevithick very well, and Mr. Brunel by reputation. Nevertheless, he was pleased that he and Jonathan had managed to see something of Trevithick's locomotive when they were in London. Fenwick was delighted that the impression it had made on him and the detail he managed to recall was of such interest to present company.

The dray hove into view with a beaming young Thomas at the reins, the drayman sitting attentively alongside. A further round of pleasantries ensued, Rosina enquiring after the well being of the older Stephenson and of Robert, George's son.

"Both well, thank ye Rosina, and all the better for you asking. Mind, the boy could do with some more meat on him. Perhaps you would take the job on?" Smiling at her puzzled expression, he went on indicating Fenwick and Matt, "As these two are so interested in steam locomotives and seem to come as a job lot, perhaps we could arrange a swap?" Fenwick and Matt could hardly contain themselves.

"Work here at Killingworth?"

"I expect to be at The Felling during this next week or early the one after. There was a meeting at the 'Lit. & Phil.' into the causes of the disaster and what might be done about safe lighting in the mine workings. I'm not promising but I'll ask if you can be released. There's a lot happening here and I could do with some willing hands an' open minds. Do y'think, Rosina, you could spare them?"

"We'd just have to manage somehow"smiled Rosina, "but I'm sure Robert will do just fine in Eleanor's good hands. Clem, we'd better be getting on our way back and pick up those two sisters at Jesmond."

"I suppose you're right, it is getting on a bit. George, we had Dr. Clanny at the John Pit talking about a safety lamp."

"A clivvor man," interjected George.

"And there's talk of Humphry Davy, now Sor Humphry Davy comin' as well."

"Noo then, there's a varry clivvor man," said George.

Rosina only just stopped herself, biting her lip, twice.

The journey home was a re-run of all the various conversations of the day and keen anticipation of what work might be in store for Matt and Fenwick at Killingworth. All anyone knew about steam locomotives was that they were great lumbering iron elephants, forever panicking cows and horses with their steam blasts and foully polluting the air with the billowing black smoke from their flame flecking stacks. They did pull prodigious loads of coal from the pitheads it was true, but they were slower than horses and frequently came off their rudimentary tracks, bringing all traffic on the roadway to a standstill. For some reason George persevered with them and it could be seen he clearly intended to continue his involvement.

The two small girls, Charlotte and Elisabeth, didn't take too long to fall asleep to the trundling of the dray and stayed that way most of the way back.

"What was that about the 'Lit. & Phil'?" asked Rosina. "I've heard about it but I don't know what it is."

"It's some sort of Club for the high-ups, but I really don't know either," said Clem.

Fenwick saw his chance. "Yes, that's what it is. A Gentleman's Club. They talk about important things, science and the like. Before the meeting starts, the Chairman sees that everyone's pipe is lit and all the glasses filled. That's where the name comes from."

Clem and Rosina glanced at each other and nodded in a silence taken as assent.

Chapter 6 - The World at Heworth

The arrangements for the mass funeral were that the remains of each victim would be taken by horse and cart from the colliery building in which they had been collected, carefully washed, and stored since their recovery from the devastated John Pit. A sombre atmosphere of quiet application had marked the undertaking of cleaning and washing each of the mortal remains. The church wardens faced a bill of historic proportions for the quantities of vinegar used as disinfectant in the cleaning of the busy toilers hands. The carpenters had long been engrossed preparing no less than ninety-two coffins of simple design but in tragically and heart-movingly differing sizes for the men and boys to be contained. These had been used to retrieve the bodies from the John Pit shaft, and respectfully lifted to bank in a net of strong cords.

In fact, only ninety-one of the known number of victims had been recovered and the identity of the final victim remains a mystery to this day. It had been a melancholy and painstaking task to ascertain identities, in many cases confirmation depending on the recognition of clothes, footwear and known personal belongings such as tobacco boxes and pocket knives.

Where possible, each cart would leave the colliery gates and pass by the victim's home, then making its own way up to the turnpike road. There it would join in the slow sad procession making its way to Heworth, the old chapel, and the waiting John Hodgson.

At each home a moments pause. A further family expression of flowers added. A slow shuffle of sad-faced relatives and friends following. Some in heart-rending despair. Some in almost silent resignation, most in dignified resolution. Tears and low murmurs of subdued talk merged with the rumbling of cartwheels on the dry stones of the roads and pathways. Each little scene was nearly identical to the next for bystanders, but heartrendingly and personally different for those trudging close behind the slowly swaying tailboards.

All over the grass green and ploughed brown sloping district landscape between the houses, beneath the mostly clear and sunlit morning sky, the grieving purposeful cohorts each made its way to join the massing and seemingly endless slow-moving column up on the turnpike road. The like of which had never been seen before and the size of which had probably not been seen on that connecting highway since Roman legions reinforced their regional stronghold at Newcastle from their supply port at South Shields or, more probably, when they effected their eventual departure from this northern, massively-walled boundary of their crumbling empire.

On arrival at the chapel each coffin was carefully laid in a bare mass grave prepared near the entrance.

Side by side, two coffins deep, a wall of lime-coated brick separated every four lying in the freshly dug ground. More lime would be added later.

'The great and the good' who had congregated in the chapel came out to join the assembly of mourners and onlookers. It seemed that every dignitary and notable for miles around was present. Clerics much senior to the Rev. John Hodgson added gravitas and some colour in their robes. Others from nearby parishes came in response to their ministry, in demonstration of their feeling for this devastated community, and out of personal regard for their scholarly and dedicated colleague. The Brandling family and many other mine owners were there. Civic delegates from near and far, local landowners, the shipping and the business communities, regional and national newspapers, were all represented. So too, in their private capacity or otherwise were members of the city of Newcastle's Literary and Philosophical Society, minds numbed by the scale of the tragedy but soberly resolved to find some future way of providing in coalmines a working light with a high level of safety. The national dismay at this horror must lead to a solution.

When the last sad container had been rested, John Hodgson addressed the huge assembly with a well-prepared and thoughtful discourse. He was keenly aware of the primary need to offer consolation to his large number of bereaved mining families. The shattering disaster in this small neighbourhood had left 41 widows and 133 orphaned children. At the same time he wanted to prompt an obligation to action in the minds of those of his listeners who had power to act or to influence working conditions now and in the future. He knew he had their attention. He knew they could but listen, and he took the opportunity to drive home their responsibilities.

As thoughts settled, he led the firm northern voices of his disparate congregation resonating in the universally known, familiar and comforting words of Psalm 22 and the Lord's Prayer.

His small local choir then valiantly rose to the occasion. They themselves decimated in the disaster, their ranks were nevertheless expanded by the turnout of a number of occasional members and sonorously augmented by the vast and attentive crowd. The old, well-known and loved hymns rang out across the sloping landscape and down to the Tyne.

Matt Robson had been watching proceedings in company with the rest of his family, standing between Fenwick and his sister, Katherine. As the crowd dispersed, he was missed. "I know where he's off to," Katherine whispered to her mother who smiled in amused agreement. "I saw him exchanging glances with Olive, the Methodist girl. The day of the explosion he thought he might get some sympathy on account of his sore shoulder but he soon found that one of her uncles was among the missing." "Poor girl," said Rosina glancing back at the mass grave ringed by mourning relatives," She'll be the one needing the sympathy this afternoon."

They made their way back to home and fireside. An awareness hung round them that their family had been extraordinarily fortunate to be spared the bleak anguish of so many of their friends and neighbours.

"Matt was saying the other day that he had a vivid dream of being swept along in a sudden underground flood and almost drowned when he had his accident just before the explosion."

"Couldn't have been that time, Katherine" said Clem. "There was no water in that part of the mine. Years ago, my father told me something like that happened to him in one of the Gateshead mines he used to work in. Water's a big problem in some parts."

"Did you ever tell him the tale?"

"Don't think so. I wouldn't want to worry him with that sort of story, would I?"

"It was probably inherited," chipped in Rosina.

"Inherited? How do you make that out?" There were times that Clem couldn't keep up with some of Rosina's strange flights of fancy. This was evidently one of them and he resolved to keep a wary distance.

"Well, we all inherit parts of our parents and grandparents, don't we? The colour of our eyes, our hair, all come down to us from them so why not memories as well?"

"Sounds a bit far-fetched to me," said Fenwick. "Perhaps you should join the 'Lit. and Phil.' and ask them. I know what. Why don't you ask the Rev. Hodgson? He might know."

"I already have," countered Rosina in the comfortable knowledge that she was one step ahead. "He said it could be possible. He had recently read something about part of the brain that does with memory. The hippo-something, I can't quite remember, but he said in fifty or a hundred years some people thought we might be able to go back through people's memories and learn all sorts. Could go back generations."

"Can't ever see that happening," said Clem.

"Well, I can," said Rosina. "Stands to reason." That terminal phrase was always an indication that further rational discussion of the subject was at an end.

Some months later she had an ideal opportunity to pursue the subject further but didn't think on, as she might have explained. She had seen the lean and studious cleric on his way up from the direction of the river and thought to put on her Sunday shoes and shawl in a quick self tidy-up just in case he called on route for the colliery offices. She was pleased she had done so as there was a knock on the door almost before she was ready.

"Good morning, Rosina. May I come in?"

"Yes, of course. Please." She motioned him inside and brought forward a chair. As he sat down, adjusting his coat tails, she covertly cast in the direction of the two small girls her family famous 'stare'. This was a warning, well known to all of her children from their earliest days, to be on their very best behaviour in the presence of 'Company'.

"How are you all?"

"We're fine thank you, as I hope you are, and we hope to see Matt and Fenwick this coming weekend."

"That's what I've called about. Fenwick. He came from Blyth didn't he? Would you ask him to call and see me? I'll be here all weekend. Sorry to be a touch mysterious, Rosina. A small private matter I need to convey to him. Nothing to be worried about."

Fenwick went over to Heworth early on the Saturday afternoon, convinced that the curious ecclesiastic summons must have something to do with his parents.

"Good afternoon, Reverend," he almost blurted. "I've always felt so guilty I didn't come home from sea earlier. Both of my parents had died before I got back, and not all that long before in my mother's case."

"Please come in and have a seat. It's not about your parents, Fenwick. We all have our regrets and you mustn't be too hard on yourself for things not all within your control. No, I wanted to see you privately about a visit I had.

A stranger called, asking for you, and I have to admit that I was somewhat less than entirely helpful to him. Let me explain. He was about my height, quite well dressed, perhaps some sort of travelling businessman, dark brown hair and a few small pockmarks on his face. His voice wasn't local, south of Yorkshire I'd say, not London, perhaps Norfolk or those parts."

Fenwick blanched and didn't want to interrupt.

"There was something in his manner which caused me a little unease. I formed the impression that he wanted me to believe that his enquiry into your whereabouts was quite casual. Indeed, to the contrary, the occasional strange movements of his hands probably indicated that he was under some stress. He must have made other enquiries because someone, doubtless having the same reservations as myself, suggested you had been lost in the John Pit disaster. I have to acknowledge that I myself sheltered behind this suggestion, confirming that one unfortunate victim had still not been found and that the total number of fatalities was variously reported in the local newspapers as 90 to 93, with the 'London Gentleman' also giving the figure as 93. He said his name was Robert Smith but declined to leave a message or a forwarding address."

"I'm certain his name is Frank Whitely, Reverend." Fenwick described the circumstances of his visit to Horncastle and his return home to Blyth. There he found his father's business sold on the basis that his parents would live rent-free in part of the chandlery and enjoy a small income for life. The new owner had produced for Fenwick a note from his father should he return, with which was enclosed a gift of ten guineas. A second letter, more recent, was from Betty Appleby painfully recounting the distressing details of Miriam's murder and the disappearance of Frank Whitely.

Fenwick had replied to her letter, intending to make a return visit to Horncastle at some time in the future. He never did. Nor did he ever learn the poignant postscript to the Appleby's story. Of course, they never recovered from their own personal kind of holocaust.

They continued to provide a warm welcome at their home to Jonathan and Miriam's many brothers and sisters and as time went by, to their children, grandchildren and numberless others besides. They lived ten years or more beyond their biblical span, celebrating the Diamond Jubilee of their wedding. At their wedding breakfast so long before, they had shared an apple, kept the core, and planted it. The resultant tree provided for countless apple pies and other tasty concoctions over the years, the mottled and distorted apples gradually showing their age as much as the admirable couple themselves in their latter years. Then, one autumn, Betty and Bill Appleby died within two weeks of each other. The orphaned apple tree blew down in a gale that very winter.

Chapter 7 - Nicola

It was like old times again for Fenwick. He got along well with Matt and they soon got heavily absorbed in their work for George Stephenson. 'Mr. Stephenson' to them both, he often paired them together on tasks though not always.

"Those two light horses, Matt. I've bought them."

"You don't hang about do you? I'll pay you back when I've got some savings put by."

"No need. We'll be able to get across to Felling most Sundays and we won't always be dependent on the colliery horses when Mr. Stephenson wants either of us to go off somewhere. An' that's happening more and more these days. I've arranged stabling at the colliery along his Irish horse 'Squire'. What shall we call ours, Matt?"

"I was thinking about that. How about 'Tinker' and 'Drummer' after those two we knew that got killed in the John Pit?"

"Suits me. Alright to call mine 'Drummer' after me navy days?"

Fenwick was right. Their own horses made them ever more useful to their far-sighted and very widely involved employer.

The Grand Allies, the powerful colliery owners consortium, thought exceedingly highly of Stephenson whose practical ability and problem solving skills made them a lot of money. Many a flooded mine was pumped dry and made to produce. In return, he was given a significant annual retainer and freedom to use workshop facilities developing his personal interests. These were generally work associated and thereby mutually beneficial.

Fenwick and Matt found themselves riding long saddle-raw hours over the coalfields of Durham and Northumberland. They checked progress and carried secondary instructions to sites following Stephenson's initial visits and analyses of problems. The man himself covered more ground, put in longer hours than anyone, and clearly had the constitution of a Bellingham ox.

Invariably, on the return of either of them he had more questions than they had thought of asking. There was never any point in giving half thought out or hopefully helpful answers as his next question would be the more difficult. He wanted straight simple answers and they soon formed the impression that his mind was usually at least half way to a solution, needing only confirmation of a point of fact here or there.

As mines went deeper seeking more profitable seams of coal to replace the old exhausted ones nearer to the surface, ever bigger and more powerful steam driven water pumps were a necessity. Our two willing and adaptable characters learned and toiled with satisfaction as new installations went up, teething troubles needed sorting and work-a-day problems presented themselves.

George's work on his safety lamp did not directly affect them but they naturally identified with this pioneering work and the locality was alive to the urgent efforts being made by Dr. Clanny, Stephenson, Sir Humphry Davy and others. They were able to throw some light, safe or otherwise, on the vexed question of some colliers perversely screwing the tops off the experimental lamps. This would gain them some additional visibility but at the expense of safety, the very purpose of the exercise.

It was clear that George Stephenson's heart and conviction was in the improvement of travelling engines, the rail riding steam locomotives. The breakthrough to the achievement of this vision came with an instruction, and adequate financial backing, from Sir Thomas Liddell for him to develop a new locomotive for the Killingworth wagon-way. At last, the chance to put his own ideas into practical action.

The immediate consequence for Matt and Fenwick was more time away from base as they attended such matters as could be delegated to them in order to give George, his brother, his son and others all the time that was possible on the development of the Stephenson locomotives.

Fenwick, however, had been hoping to spend rather more time at Killingworth. Whenever he had the opportunity, certainly when he was on his own, he had taken to passing by a certain house in Jesmond. This was the house he and his relatives had called at on their way to his first meeting with George Stephenson. The two Heworth sisters had been seen off, on their way back, by a coterie of relatives and friends including their young and attractive cousin, Nicola.

Several years younger than Fenwick, she certainly caught his eye on that occasion but it was some time before he contrived the opportunity to remind her of their previous meeting. She was a bright, independently minded girl. Dark hair, grey-brown eyes in a round, serious pale face which easily broke into a smile he remembered well and hoped one day to see again.

He couldn't raise the courage just to knock on the front door and have done with it. Cannon fire was almost as daunting. He would slowly ride past, trying not to be noticed, but hoping for some glimpse of her even obscurely and distantly perhaps through a part curtained window. Eventually, he resorted to wandering towards the Sunday morning mass at St. Andrews in the reasonable hope of seeing her there. The pretext he used for his absence from Clem and Rosina's at Felling was to attend the crowded Newcastle quayside market not far from the church.

Then suddenly it happened. He hadn't given up hope exactly, but he was despairing of seeing her again on her own. Perhaps she had left the district or was now spoken for. One Sunday morning, on another fake visit to the quayside market, he happened to go up to the church rather later than had been usual for him. Most of the congregation were out and on their way home or heading down in the direction of the bridge and the riverside market. Some stragglers were cheerily chatting among themselves and he noticed a fresh group spilling out into the street, Nicola among them.

He caught her eye immediately and, with a confidence that surprised himself, walked over introducing himself and reminding her of their first rather brief meeting. She said she remembered him and sensitively didn't say that truthfully she remembered Matt somewhat more. Seizing the moment, as he could see she was looking hesitantly towards a waiting coach, he asked if he could call to see her.

Slightly taken back and off balance by this precipitate request, she found herself asking when he might be passing again through Jesmond.

"Next Sunday afternoon?"

"I'll tell my parents you'll be calling."

She swished off in her Sunday best, leaving Fenwick blinking in his Sunday luck, feeling at least a foot taller and his chest tight as a drum.

The following week was a blur. Fortunately perhaps, there was such a lot going on at work that he didn't have too much time to think. It was almost the weekend before he confided in Matt, not that he wanted to be secretive and, anyway, Rosina's antennae would be sure soon to home in on his fairly evident distraction.

He was made welcome at Jesmond and got to know Nicola's parents and two of her brothers. She had an older sister living out, and another brother enlisted with his Regiment, serving in the borders.

Nicola Martin was by now working in her uncle's shipping and transport office, just off Newcastle's quayside along by Trinity House. Her uncle was by far the richer of the two brothers and lived in a large well-appointed house in its own grounds above Jesmond Dene. In a good clear hand she wrote out letters from his drafts and her attractive presence around his offices was a welcome feature to many a visitor. Her ability to draft some letters herself and her assured discretion and confidentiality made her much appreciated by her uncle.

Fenwick realised he was talking quite a lot about his work in George Stephenson's employ but remembered not to elaborate too much on his epic heroism helping out Admiral Collingwood at Trafalgar and in the more local and recent John Pit disaster. Nicola's mother had stopped plying him with scones and was saying that Nicola mustn't take up too much of his Sunday time and perhaps they would see him again soon. He made his goodbyes and Nicola saw him to the door.

Her face told him she was pleased with his visit. He wasn't at all certain that the pleasure was wholly in seeing him or, because of his visit she was in a new way the current focus of attention in her family, or possibly a bit of both.

"I'd like to call on you again, Nicola?"

"I think that might be chanced." At least the rejoinder came with a ready smile, so that was all right.

"I'll be away for at least the next two weeks down at Darlington. Fingers crossed everything will go well. Will you be at St. Andrews again?"

" I'm there every Sunday."

"Oh. I've stopped there quite a few times hoping to see you. You never seemed to be inside the church or coming out with the crowd afterwards."

Another amused smile. "I'll let you into a little secret. That's because I'm upstairs, and the choir always come out last."

"Oh! I didn't realise that you sang."

"A little. We're a bit of a musical family. Careful you don't get roped in. I enjoy the company of the choir. They're a good crowd. I sang solo with them when I was sixteen. Midnight Mass. I was terrified, but it went alright."

"I'll know to stay a little longer next time, and hope to see you when you come out."

- o O o -

The Stockton to Darlington Railway had been a great public success but the far-seeing George wasn't altogether satisfied.

'His' rails were being obliged to carry a mixture of traffic. 'His' travelling engines were being impeded by carriages and coaches drawn by horses. The laying down of stretches of single tracks for economy and then providing insufficient passing places had led to many a heated argument over right of way. There were fights between the drivers. There were the additional complications of occasional steep inclines where the traffic was pulled up by ropes from fixed engines. These caused bottlenecks on normal days and total chaos when those engines failed or the ropes snapped.

His vision was of locomotives leading passengers and goods from town terminus to town terminus on near level rails and no horses in the way at all.

"Are they all giants?" asked Tommy.

"Who, son?"

Saturday evenings were becoming a regular family convergence for a good meal prepared by Rosina, ample ale and lemonade, followed by bread and cheese unlimited and the opportunity for everyone to help put the world to rights. Visitors were welcomed with warmth and soon found themselves inveigled into taking sides on whatever issue was under discussion. The more perceptive soon realised that Clem was quietly enjoying his promotion of conversational controversies and often found themselves defending the very views they recalled opposing on their last visit. Rosina, ever alert to the sensitivities of the guests under her roof, would take sides with them whatever the debate, when she felt her husband's whimsical humour was in the remotest danger of crossing the bounds of hospitality.

"Locomotive men. Mr. Stephenson is a canny big man. I've heard tell that Richard Trevithick from Cornwall was the biggest man ever seen in Gateshead and Timothy Hackworth seems even bigger than Mr. Stephenson. What about Mr. Brunel, Fenwick?"

"Not as I remember, Tommy, but then I wasn't very old myself when I was at Chatham. His son might be tall though. He's only a couple or so years younger than young Mr. Robert and works with his father as an engineer, just like Robert."

"They drink even more than the Sunderland colliers."

"Who?"

"Cornishmen."

"Whoever told you that?"

"One of the men down at the yard. Will travelling engines ever go as fast as horses?"

"Perhaps. They can certainly pull heavier loads than horses ever can. On well-laid rails they really can get up to a fair old speed.

That's the thing. They're always coming off bad rails, and they do need to be level. Mr. Stephenson says straight and level as possible. If you come to a hill don't climb it. Go round it on the level, or cut a passage through it, or tunnel under it. Always keep as near level as possible."

"They'll never go as fast as horses", opined Rosina passing through from the kitchen. "Great lumbering noisy metal elephants. Spouting steam and frightening the horses and cattle."

"Why ever not?" queried Clem.

"It stands to reason."

Chapter 8 – Trouble at Liverpool

Young Robert Stephenson had returned from his short stint at Edinburgh University and was wholly committed to his father's vision of travelling engines travelling everywhere without self-centred let or prejudiced hindrance. The big opportunity after Stockton was the new way Parliament wanted laid from Manchester to Liverpool. Already the canal couldn't carry anywhere near the amount of traffic the new industries were producing.

Ever more miles in the saddle resulted for George but, to his mind, there was also the good compensation of healthy fresh air for the physically less robust Robert. Fifty miles of survey work were eventually all but completed and George's ideas almost in place.

"Fenwick. I want you and Matt to go to Liverpool. That section we talked about through the Earl's land needs checking. You know how much he opposes our line or any line through his property. I'm too well known in those parts by now. So is my brother and for that matter, young Robert. You'll need to be very careful. I've heard the Earl has hired men with guns whose job it is to see off anyone and everything to do with railways or surveys. If you find it's too difficult, come back. It will take time but we can always get an order through the Magistrates."

Matt had proposed to his Methodist girl and was now looking about for a more settled job. He knew that George Stephenson had put in a word for him with the influential Charles Brandling. Ideally, this would lead to some job on the south side of the Tyne and soon. The present foray into the Liverpool area, he earnestly hoped, would be his last protracted absence. Olive was a lovely, intelligent, fresh-faced, straw haired, quietly organised sort of girl who couldn't wait to set up her own home and start her new life. Rosina had taken to her immediately. She was the one love of Matt's life and he was devoted to her, equally longing for the start of their new life together.

He and Fenwick found lodgings a few miles out of Liverpool. Under the guise of seeking wood supplies for the collieries of the Grand Allies, they were able to roam the area with little question. They visited the Liverpool dock offices where Irish timber could be bought, showed themselves at some of the inland forests owned by the higher gentry and, in particular, the woodlands owned by the ill-disposed, obstreperous, and certainly ungracious Earl.

They had decided to use assumed names and, not being practised in the deceptive arts, quite often found themselves struggling in strange company to avoid the use of their own proper names. Somehow they managed and felt smugly satisfied with their caution one evening in the vicinity of the terrain they had come to check.

Matt had gone down to the local alehouse, ahead of Fenwick who was feeding and watering 'Drummer' and 'Tinker' before securing them for the night. When they were on their own, eating, Matt indicated the group of men at the bar he had been talking to when Fenwick arrived.

"They were going on about the Earl's hired press gang. A few of them have guns; the others have staves and know how to use them. They'll crack a few heads if need be, and not think twice about it. The Earl has been approached by all of the railway companies for surveys through his lands and has turned them all down. He's dead against every one of them. He won't hear tell of anything to do with the railways and says he will fight the militia if the government insist on giving people wayleaves through any part of his property. Two of that group were looking about for rabbits and ended up with a beating and a warning. Lucky they had nothing on them or they'd have been in serious trouble."

"We were well warned."

"Perhaps that's not the half of it."

"What d'you mean?"

"None of the hired gang are local. The fellow in charge is a nasty piece of work. Wait 'til you hear this. They said his name was Robert or Bob Smith. Wasn't that the name of the man that you were warned about by the Reverend Hodgson?"

"Hell's flames! It's an ordinary enough name, Matt, but you're probably right." Fenwick was stunned into a momentary and uncharacteristically thoughtful silence.

"So what do we do now?"

"Let's think. I don't know about you but I want to get this job finished. George needs this information without hanging about waiting for official permits, and he's been very good to us."

"I agree. We could take a leaf out of George's own book and take our check survey on Sunday morning when the Earl and his staff are all in their chapel. We've got all we needed to know about the river flood levels. Then again, I don't suppose Smith and his gang are likely to be attending chapel anyway."

"No, but they may be a bit more off guard. Hopefully after a heavy Saturday night. Let's plan to finish off on Sunday morning and get back out of this place."

They were out on site by dawn on the Sunday morning. The early morning dew saturated their boots and leggings in no time. No matter, it couldn't be helped. They would dry out before too long when the sun rose a bit. The section to be check-surveyed closely followed the river and was mostly on the Earl's land. The final stretch would bring them up to a public road where they would have relative safety.

Taking the levels was a two-man job, but, as one jotted down the readings and made notes, the other would ride up the nearest hill to scan the countryside for signs of the Earl's private militia. Matt did see some riders at a distance just before they were about to move on to take what would be the last readings they needed. These they managed to take and note in some haste. Soon, both were glad to be on the highway heading back to their lodgings. Perversely, this also happened to be in the general direction of the Earl's impressive residence. Almost immediately they were accosted by two of his men clearly having set out from it not long before.

"Whoa!" An imperious hand obliged them to stop and suspicious eyes roamed with satisfaction over the survey equipment lashed over the hindquarters of their horses.

"Surveying for the railway are you?" No attempt was made to disguise an air of confident menace in the question.

"Not a bit of it," responded Fenwick as coolly as he could. "Who would do such work on the Sabbath?" Why not brazen it out? It was only two against two, anyway. "We're travelling to see Mr. Thompson, the Earl's land steward for leave to start a survey tomorrow morning and, yes, for one of the railway companies."

"You're wasting your time. There's no chance of that. You come along o'me and Mr. Thompson will tell you himself."

There was little they could do but comply, Fenwick dreading the prospect and consequences of being confronted by Frank Whitely, alias Robert or Bob Smith, with all those implications. Apart from his own safety he feared for Matt and felt responsible for putting him into a double danger so near to his wedding.

Thompson was equally suspicious and carefully wrote down their names and that of their lodgings for the night. "No consents at all are being given here for wayleaves and surveys. Anyway, Mr. Smith has responsibility for that sort of thing, and he isn't here today. He'll probably want to see you himself tomorrow so I'll bid you good day and ask you to leave these grounds immediately."

Suppressing huge sighs of relief they remounted and rode off without speaking, as calmly and as quickly as they dared.

Going back to their lodgings they settled up, packed their belongings, then headed north and east in the direction of Newcastle. They took very good care indeed to avoid any further chance of trespass on the Peer's substantial but hostile territory.

"Thank the Lord the madman Whitely wasn't around. He's certain to make enquiries tomorrow and be very suspicious we've left. All the better we used false names." They were still chuckling happily to themselves when they stopped at nightfall at a reassuringly remote hostelry.

"Why should we be chucked off his land like that?" demanded an aggrieved Matt, washing his face in the hand basin on the chest of drawers.

"Because it's his land and he's got the law on his side. Don't use all the water in that jug."

"You'll probably tell me I'm sounding like Tom Paine again, but he probably got his land from the King or more likely a previous one," said Matt drying his face and airing his argument with equal vigour. "Perhaps even going back to William the Conqueror. Ownership by force of arms. That can't be right."

"Right or wrong, Matt. That's the law and there's nothing you or I can do about it. If you try, you'll end up in serious trouble. Look what happened to your Tom Paine."

"So nothing gets done, out of fear." Matt had the bit between his teeth and wasn't inclined to let go. "People on the land pay rent and tithes to the landed gentry for nothing more than to scratch a living for themselves. Any wonder the French and the Americans wouldn't put up with it any longer?"

"I'm not sure they've ended up with anything better. Perhaps the land has just ended up in different hands. Anyway, the Frenchies and the Americans are different to us. I can't see us using the guillotine on our gentry and the Americans just wanted a fresh start. Best not to rock the boat or you'll get yourself a reputation, Matt."

Matt's wedding was the highlight of the family year. The Rev. Hodgson's sterling efforts at the time of the disaster and afterwards, together with his steadily growing reputation as a local historian of some distinction made him well known throughout the locality. He had set to with his characteristic determination to rebuild the crumbling old chapel at Heworth and had succeeded in replacing it with a truly splendid new parish church of St. Mary's.

Olive, however, wanted her wedding to take place in her modest and familiar Methodist chapel down Felling Shore where she and Matt had met years before in the furtherance of their equally modest but prized education.

Fenwick ran into somewhat similar problems with Nicola. Although they were not as yet exactly 'going out' he had not considered she would demur at his invitation to Matt's wedding where he was to be best man.

"I'm sorry, I couldn't do that," she said. "As a Catholic I couldn't attend a service in a church or chapel of another religion."

"Why not?"

"We aren't allowed to. We never accepted the changes of the Reformation and we stay with the old faith, not recognising any others. Won't you have a problem going to the Methodist chapel? Has Matt become a Methodist now? How about you?"

"We've never discussed these things. I'm not fixed to any church or chapel. I don't see the difference and the old religious restrictions seem to have been going since we had John Wesley in these parts. And now there's talk of emancipating or whatever, the Irish and possibly you English Catholics."

Nicola looked pre-occupied. "I do wish Matt and Olive every happiness, I really do. They make such a nice couple and I'm sure Rev. Hodgson will wish them well too."

The wedding indeed went well. Olive was as radiant as every bride should be and her parent's home was bursting all the day long with well-wishers. The young couple immediately settled into their new home above the Turnpike road, between Felling Hall and the new St. Mary's, Matt having been offered and settled for a leading engineman's position at the reopened and once more thriving colliery.

At Killingworth the pace of life and work stepped up with a gusto. On top of an already busy and widespread workload, the Stephensons had thrown themselves with energy and total enthusiasm into the challenge of an unprecedented and unexpected competition.

The arguments had raged it seemed for years. Horses or travelling engines? A mixture of the two on roads or on rails? A mixture of moving engines on mostly level ground and some fixed ones to help traffic up serious inclines?

There was a hotchpotch of convictions. As is often the case with hotly disputed arguments, the most heated opinions were propelled by those with little or no visible logic to their thoughts nor any relevant backing experience. Then again, the wildest assertions get credence with repetition and it becomes ever harder to clear the ground and square up to the essentials.

George Stephenson never had any doubts. The Directors of the 'Liverpool & Manchester' in his view were a godsend. Their recognition of the basic problems and their willingness to identify solutions in open display was a challenge George relished and took up with all of his wholehearted and formidable vigour.

The Board of Directors offered no less than a prize sum of £500 for a travelling engine to meet their requirements in a competition open to all-comers. Over and above the distinction of the initial prize, the winner could expect significant orders for supplies of his successful machine for the new railway. The race or ordeal or trial would be held at Rainhill, near to Liverpool, under the strictest of conditions. These would relate to the amount of fuel and water used, measured against distance and speed travelled. Basic measurable facts.

Would the travelling engines, locomotives, be up to it?

The gauntlet was picked up at Killingworth with enthusiasm. It was also picked up the length and breadth of the country by serious engineers and by unmitigated crackpots alike. For every possible contender capable of producing a credible design, or improving on an existing one, there were a hundred fanciful opportunists similarly stimulated. Out came the cherished schemes for perpetual motion and every nascent conception to solve mankind's transport problems. The admirable Board didn't know what had come to hit them.

"We'll need something a touch lighter and a lot faster than any of our existing engines. Speed but still strength and pulling power. That's the way Mr. Stephenson is thinking. He and Robert have a lot of ideas and we'll come up with something special. Don't worry about that."

"Who else will be a serious runner? Is Richard Trevithick no longer interested? And what are they doing down at Leeds now?"

"This would have been right up Trevithick's street, no mistake. Haven't heard of him in a long time, Clem. Leeds Middleton might be interested though. What's going on elsewhere in the country I really don't know. I'm sure George and Robert will hear bits and pieces through their business contacts. One thing you can be sure of, there will be lots of interest in London if only to spite George. This engine competition is the talk of the country and there's plenty down there who won't want George to win. They seem to regard him as an uneducated clod who speaks a foreign language anyway.

I reckon a serious competitor for us will be much nearer home, at Shildon here in County Durham. Timothy Hackworth is a first class engineer as everyone knows from working with him at Killingworth. Very interested in locomotives and from what I hear, wouldn't be against putting one over on George himself."

"Sounds like you're in for a bit of a scrap. Will you be much involved?"

" I haven't been so far. But there's no telling what can happen at Killingworth."

"What's happening with Nicola?" Rosina had heard enough about travelling engines. "Are we allowed to ask?"

"Of course you are. She's very well thank you. Still working hard in her uncle's office."

"And?"

There was no escaping. "I still see her from time to time".

"But?"

Fenwick knew he was cornered. Rosina was being as blunt and direct as only very few close friends and close relatives, especially female ones, can be. He readily understood her concern for him but hadn't recognised that her natural protective instincts for her immediate family included him more deeply than he had been aware. The persistence of her questions came not from simple curiosity but from an intuitive apprehension for his person and feelings.

"I'm not sure her parents think I'm the right person for her".

"What makes you think that?"

"They're polite and all that. Just…a bit distant, and I know I'm not the cleverest at working out what's in people's minds unless they come out and tell me directly."

"If you sense something's there, it quite possibly is. What do you think it might be?"

Fenwick paused for thought.

"They're a fairly well-to-do family. Big house as you know. The uncle is very rich. Perhaps they want her to do better and I'm very sure she could. I just don't work with and meet up with the sort of people they mix with.

There are times I can see they are trying to bring me into the conversation and I'm struggling to say something of any relevance at all. One time they were talking about the Lake District and William Wordsworth and poetry. I've only just about heard his name. Me, I'd know a lot more about Jim Belcher and Tom Cribb and prize fighting. Nicola does say things to include me but perhaps I'm just plain out of my depths with these people."

"Have you talked to her to see what she thinks?"

"Not really, but you're right. I need to."

Chapter 9 - More Trouble

"How long have you been seeing this young man, Nicola?"

It was a bright and mild Saturday afternoon in November. The live-in maid was out on an errand and Mrs. Georgina Martin had the house, and her youngest daughter, all to herself. She hadn't been looking forward to this somewhat difficult conversation but she was convinced that it was necessary. An auburn haired, now homely woman, attractive in her time she knew her place in the world and was respected in her part of it for the support she gave her husband and all of her family. True, she would have welcomed a larger income, certainly in their earlier years, but what of it? She always was blessed with enough common sense, she felt, to get her priorities right and to see her family grow in health and sanity as the years went by.

"You know how long, mother, and his name is Fenwick." Nicola had suspected for some time that an uneasy dialogue with her mother was in the offing. She gently smoothed her thick green and black Irish tartan skirt and tried to look relaxed.

"You know what I mean."

Mrs. Martin felt hugely relieved that the conversation was under way. It was an effort to ease her shoulders downwards and at the same time reduce the pressure in her lungs that suddenly seemed far too full and expanded.

"Yes, I do know what you mean. You don't approve? You don't really like him do you, and you don't think he's *suitable!*" The words rather tumbled out and Nicola felt she was speaking more sharply to her mother than she ever intended. Her hands were gripping her knees so she folded them more easily in her lap.

"Nicola dear, I do quite like him but you are still young and I do worry that you may be getting involved with someone you don't know all that much about and who you don't have all that much in common with."

"You mean he never went to proper school and doesn't come from the same sort of people we know. Well, I like him. I like him a lot. He's open and honest with me in everything he says and does. He's a natural gentleman even if he hasn't been born and educated like one. I always enjoy being with him. He's interesting and amusing and he's been through more experiences in life than most of the people that we know."

Mrs. Martin was breathing more easily now. "I don't question that he doesn't have many good qualities but your father and I are concerned that you may be embarking on a friendship which may not lead to our little daughter's happiness, and that is all we want."

"I'm not your little daughter any more, *mother*. Doesn't papa like Fenwick?"

"I'm sure he quite likes him as well, but we share the same concerns for you. We had a discussion and he thought it best that you and I had a little talk first."

"Mama, you're making this sound serious!"

"It's meant to be sensible, Nicola. This is the first young man you have shown any real interest in and, where personal feelings are concerned, it is all too easy to get carried away on the whims of the moment and suffer regrets later. Now Fenwick doesn't share our faith and there may well be other differences that haven't yet shown themselves." She paused and took a breath. "Your father will be telling you he has decided that you should stop seeing this young man, at least until after your next birthday."

"Mama, no. That's not until nearly the end of September next!"

"Time may or may not be important." Georgina Martin had not been certain how this dictat would be received and was relieved the reaction wasn't stronger. Nicola was clearly hurting and coping with some stress. She put her arms around her and gave her a squeeze as she had so often done. "There are many things to consider. To begin with, your Catholic faith is important to you, is it not?"

"Of course. Fenwick has no objections to our faith. He's told me so."

"That's not the same thing now, is it? When push comes to shove, it might be a different matter entirely. Now don't get upset, Nicola dearest. Papa and I love you very much and all we want is for your lifelong happiness. One day, I'm sure you will see this is the right thing to do. You must tell Fenwick the next time you see him, or write to him, and if he truly cares for you I'm sure he will agree."

Nicola said nothing more in her morose and pensive silence as her mother got up, pressed her shoulder and with a sympathetic smile, left her to her thoughts.

The following morning there was a light but steady drizzle which prompted Fenwick to drop Drummer's reins over a convenient railing spike while he himself took shelter in the ample doorway of St. Andrew's. It wouldn't be long before the Mass was over and Nicola would come smiling out. Already some of the packed congregation, habitual occupiers of the very crowded back of the sturdy church, were on their way out earnestly hurrying to doubtless pressing business in one of the nearby taverns or hostelries.

He stood, back to the entrance wall, like a stranded pebble on the shore as the tide of men, women and children, flowed past him breaking into cheerful close conversations and grimacing upwards at the unfriendly skies.

Her smile of recognition was brief and she took his hand, moving him away from the cluster of people buttoning their own and children's coats, putting up hoods, and generally preparing to face the inclement journey home.

"Nicola." He kissed her cheek, considering that particular demonstration of affection wouldn't be out of place on church premises. "Something the matter?" One look at her face clearly told him there was.

"We need to have a talk, Fenwick. My parents feel we are seeing too much of each other and want me to stop seeing you at least until after my next birthday, which isn't until almost the end of next September." She hesitated, a forlorn look on her pale face such as he'd never seen before.

He pulled her to him. "Oh no. No. Surely not? I haven't really seen all that much of you, being away such a lot of the time …but I've felt something wasn't right for a while. You know how much you mean to me, Nicola. There's no one in the whole world who means more to me. I suppose I've been so pleased to get to know you and to be with you I haven't given time for much thought to anything else.

Look. You have to go now, and I'm expected back by Rosina and Clem. I'll ride over later this afternoon. We can talk more then. I won't stay to dinner or anything but please ask your father if he would see me. I think I know him well enough now not to come to blows." He raised a smile and won the faintest of smiles back. "Bye for now sweetheart."

She walked over to the waiting coach, somewhat slowly and deep in thoughts that failed to make orderly sense no matter how hard she tried.

Fenwick wasn't smiling as he rode over that afternoon and, although the rain had stopped, his spirits hadn't lifted or brightened with the skies.

He took his horse round to the back of the house, leaving the lightly sweating animal saddled as he didn't know how long he might be, but contentedly munching on some hay. Nicola came out to greet him and he could see she had been crying. "Papa will see you straight away, and you must promise to see me before you .. leave."

"I promise," he said, thinking she sensitively chose 'leave' over 'go'.

Malcolm Martin was an industrious man, no longer as lithe and athletic as he had been and never as commercially perceptive as his eldest brother. However he had made use of his education and had made steady progress in the commercial insurance market growing on Tyneside. He slowly paced his study, not quite being certain of what he was going to say. There was a light knock on the panelled door and the maid announced "Mr. Skipsey."

"Come in son."

He motioned Fenwick to a chair while he remained standing. This was partly automatic as such was his custom when giving office instructions to his staff. It was also a preference on the older man's part as he knew he wouldn't be comfortable sitting down to say what he had to say, and if he should find himself shifting from one foot to the other he could at least move about.

"How are you?"

"Well, thank you." Fenwick made no effort to add to the somewhat strained and formal exchange of pleasantries.

Mr. Martin cleared his throat which didn't need clearing and came straight to the point. "Nicola's mother and I are concerned that the friendship you and our daughter have recently struck up may not be appropriate to her best interests at this present time." He looked across at Fenwick who was focussed on him with rapt attention. "She is young and, while you are certainly a few years older in the calendar, you have very much more experience than she has of the wider world. We feel that more time is needed for her to develop her interests without the inevitable and quite restrictive constraints of an exclusive friendship." He paused, feeling just a little bit pleased and frankly relieved to have got this said in orderly fashion.

"Appropriate?" None of the other words jarred like this one. Fenwick could accept, even agree, with the others in the circumstances. At the same time he knew in his bones that there were two basic objections to him in the minds of this family. No matter how they dressed them up. He didn't come from their business background and he wasn't a Catholic. Face up to it.

The word, the question, the objection, hung in the air with the smell of the coal fire, the cut flowers, and the furniture polish. Appropriate! For a moment neither of the two men spoke. Then Fenwick did.

"I know we come from different backgrounds. I know that others will have more to offer than perhaps I ever will but Nicola means more to me than anything in my life and I'd do anything for her. We have only known each other really for a few months and a lot of the time I've been working miles away. She's a wonderful girl to be with and I haven't thought beyond the present, Mr. Martin. Perhaps I should have. Are you saying that you want me to stop calling on Nicola altogether?"

"I haven't said that."

"Nicola did tell me that you wanted us to part until next September. Do you really want us to part altogether and not just until then? You and Mrs. Martin have always made me very welcome here but I know that Nicola will be able to meet others with much better prospects than me. Or is there something else?"

Malcolm Martin slightly opened his mouth but paused before answering, and reflectively stroked his chin between his left thumb and forefinger. He sat down, not behind his desk but in a chair near to where Fenwick was sitting beside a bureau.

He leant forward. "I think we understand each other. You may do well in your life. I hope you do. You work hard and with good people in rising businesses. There is a lot happening in this part of the country and I think there may well be opportunities for you. I won't pretend that good prospects aren't of importance to any father of daughters. Now, you ask if there is something else. There is, of course.

You know we are a catholic family. Have been for many years. Not quite the problem it was in the penal times but there are still difficulties and disadvantages to be overcome. There are signs these days that official barriers will fall but I fear that in high and influential places the old resentments and handicaps will continue. I know that you don't share these antagonisms but you must be aware of them."

Fenwick nodded.

"People lose jobs or don't get jobs or business they should and the pressures to conform are all around. Those of us who have kept the ancient faith of this country, and those who have had the courage and conviction to adopt it, well know the pitfalls. I know that Nicola is firm in her faith and, young as she is, is prepared to make any sacrifice that comes her way. I don't expect others to have the same views on many matters and that is where conflict can arise. True, you don't share our faith and that puts limits to where minds can meet.

"I do consider that it would be in everyone's best interests if you both had time to reflect. I don't believe that a total ban would be a civilised position to take and that is why I have instructed Nicola to end your association at least until after her next birthday. I do understand and very much regret that this will be hurtful to you but I hope that you can understand that I act in what I believe to be Nicola's best interests."

He paused to let his words sink in, feeling some sympathy for the downcast face in front of him staring hopelessly at the carpet pattern.

"Can I have your assurance that you accept my decision?"

After a moment, Fenwick straightened himself and stood up. "If that is what you and Mrs. Martin really want I won't go against you. I don't know what I can do but I won't be the cause of trouble between yourselves and Nicola. I think too much of her for that and she really is important to me."

Turning away and opening the study door, he asked in a flat and none too steady voice, "Alright if I speak to Nicola before I leave?"

Nicola's father nodded.

Retrieving his cape from the hallstand, he was wondering how to locate Nicola when she appeared from one door and the housemaid from another. The maid nodded and left. "I'll walk you to the stable" murmured Nicola, almost in a whisper and moving to open the yard door before he could speak. She swung a dark brown shawl over the shoulders of her cream patterned Sunday dress which precaution was just as well in the chill of the late afternoon and fading wintery light. Instinctively, she had fastened the shawl with the ornamental concentric rings fashioned from some shark's backbone and given to her by Fenwick.

They went into the stable where Drummer perked up on seeing them. Clinging despairingly to each other in a warm but bemused embrace, it was Nicola who spoke first, and apprehensively.

"Was papa horrible to you?"

"Not really, no my sweet. I'm still feeling numb and hollow and don't know what to think." She squeezed him with a sympathetic hug.

"What are we going to do?" asked Fenwick blankly, knowing full well that any answers had to come from him.

"I know this much. I'm not giving up on you and I hope you wouldn't want me to." Her pale but steady smile thankfully did not indicate any form of dissent. "I can see where their worries come from and your father was quite fair, really. I couldn't have put it as well myself if I tried." He sighed and very slightly shook his head in an effort to clear his thoughts. Miserably and desperately, he knew he had to come to some conclusion. Some understanding had to be made with his Nicola before he parted from her, here and now, this very afternoon.

"I won't go against your parents, and I don't want you to be estranged from them in any way. They believe they are doing what's best for you." Nicola had leant back from him, dismay in her face. "Listen, my sweet. I'm going to keep my word and I'm going to keep your father to his. I can't see any way round this otherwise without the cause of a lot of bad feeling. Perhaps I can prove to him that at least some of his fears are groundless."

"But next September is almost a year away!" The despair in her voice couldn't be hidden. "Perhaps I could come to see you. We can write." She was casting around in a hopeless agony for some vaguely palatable alternative.

"I've given my word, my love, and if I set sail along those lines I'd feel I was up to some deceit."

"Well, I haven't given my word on anything. I don't care for any of their objections, and don't tell me that's just petulance."

"All right I won't. But it is." He smiled to win her over, but without success.

"Look. Next September seems a long way away but the time will pass and you will be all the more precious to me when it does. Also, who knows, your parents might decide I'm quite a wonderful fellow after all."

This time she did concede a reluctant smile.

"What makes you so sure I'll still be here to come back to?"

"I suppose I'll have to take a chance on that!"

Both hearts missed a beat at the harrowing thought even expressed in banter.

It was getting cold. His hands certainly were. His cape was taking some care of hers and he moved his hands up from the small of her back towards her shoulders and under the warmth of her shawl. Much better.

She turned her face as he did so and he bent towards her lips. He was moved by a yearning to be with this captivating young woman who had taken him over in a way no one ever had. How could he be parting from her?

He kissed her tenderly and held her close, breathing in her femininity. Her soft perfume, the simple scent of her clothes, her simple nearness, all but intoxicated him. Her lips then pressed on his with an ardent warmth he had never before experienced. Not from her or from anyone. He responded instantly. Two bodies relished their closeness and their arms clung on to the moment as much as their lips. She pulled away first, putting a finger to his lips and saying "I must go" with a slight, slow, shake of her head. Handing him Drummer's bridle she pushed on the stable door and stood wistfully as Fenwick slowly led out his horse and climbed the stirrup. He turned the horse, bent down to kiss her upturned lips lightly once more and rode off, a sombre glance back and left arm part raised in a farewell salute until he was forlornly far out of her sight.

Chapter 10 - Hard work never killed anyone

She was never far from his thoughts no matter where he was. Fenwick was aware of his loneliness in a way he had never known before. He got along with most people and enjoyed the mannish banter of the workplace wherever he was. It wasn't the same any more though. The expeditions from time to time with Matt were no longer there and he had no other friends he could regard as close. For the first time in his life he was all too often separated from his familiar, busy, ofttimes cramped and crowded throng of crew or colliers.

This wasn't the Stephensons' problem, of course, but in a not too roundabout way they provided the solution. The pace of work stepped up again. The new fast locomotive was certainly the focus of attention for both George and his capable and scholarly son, but nothing else was neglected. If Fenwick wasn't away in his usual role of go-between at seemingly every pithead operation in these northern parts of His Majesty's kingdom, he was increasingly involved in the development activities at base Killingworth and at the new Forth Banks factory in Newcastle.

Truth to tell, there had not been all that many opportunities for himself and Matt to get closely involved in either the running or the making of the Stephenson steam locomotives which had attracted them in the first place. At every chance, however, in their variety of supporting roles they had involved themselves where they could. In his new even less confined circumstances Fenwick now found himself taking every possibility to learn and to familiarise himself with the operation and the problems of these powerful trundling machines.

At Killingworth on quiet days and the driver in a good humour he would manage rides on the precarious narrow footboard facing across the boiler, the driver on his precarious narrow footboard. In the latter's case, the degree of hazard was increased by the proximity of the array of shafts and valve handles from which he contrived to control the steaming beast. The fireman's job was simpler, though not without its own dangers as he shovelled coal into the hungry furnace while standing on a swaying coal-strewn tender. Fenwick soon got the hang of that job, judging the state of the fire and the amount of coal to put in to keep up the head of steam.

Driving was much more difficult but he found that he had something of a latent capability for it. The swaying, jolting vehicle wasn't just quite the same thing as clinging on to a yardarm and trying to do a repair in a boisterous gale but there were similarities. It certainly needed some skill. It needed balance and dexterity and he found that he had a natural aptitude and judgement for driving and braking. He had to admit though, he never proficiently mastered the high art of manipulating the valves and reversing the machine. Only the best drivers could do that well. In a similar fashion he had learned to ride quite well but would never regard himself as a first class horse rider.

Drummer learned some new skills too. All over the countryside there were horse drawn rail wagons for transporting coal to the collier boats. The coalmines were generally uphill from the rivers so the loaded coal wagons would go downhill by gravity and would be brought back empty uphill by a horse. In many places the horse would be provided with a dandy cart in which it would ride and eat at its leisure, at the end of the line of coal wagons on the downward journey. More than once, Fenwick cajoled an apprehensive and clattering Drummer into a dandy cart to take advantage of a speedier downhill journey. It is doubtful if the four-legged passenger found this alternative form of transport relaxing.

Many a time on his way from Killingworth to the Stephensons' new locomotive works at Forth Banks, Newcastle, Fenwick was tempted to detour by Nicola's home in Jesmond. He never did though. The prospect of being seen and caught out like a small boy in an orchard with an armful of fruit was deterrent enough, and he had given his word. Very soon he heard that Nicola had been sent down to London by her father so there was no point to the detour anyway.

Forth Banks wasn't all that far from St. Andrews and the Tyne Bridge so it was just a relatively short ride to Rosina and Clem's at The Felling.

"What news of the new locomotive, Fenwick?"

"It's been quite a struggle but they're getting there. There's been all sorts of problems and both George and Robert have been spending all the hours God sends trying this and that. Getting the new boiler right was driving the yard to distraction, believe me."

"The Rev. Hodgson says it was in the newspapers that it's been taken out on trials and that it's very fast. They say it goes like a Congreve rocket. Is that what they're going to call it?"

"The Rev. is very well informed as usual, Tommy. It's going to be called the *Rocket*."

"Will it win the competition?"

"We think so, and George seems to have no doubts. The London newspapers favour the *Novelty* but Timothy Hackworth at Shildon is my biggest fear."

"Are you likely to be involved in the trials at Liverpool?"

"I didn't think so, but this last week I was sent for and I might be. The *Rocket* is to be dismantled and packed onto wagons to be taken to Carlisle and shipped to Liverpool. The transport is being arranged by Nicola's uncle's company, would you believe it, and George wants me to go with the wagons and make sure that nothing is lost or damaged on the way."

"Any more news of Nicola?"

"Not really, Rosina. So far as I know, she is still with the family of a friend her uncle knows down in Kensington. This friend is to do with the Royal

Geographical Society and Nicola was helping out there and being taken all over the place during the London season."

"Where's Kensington?"

"Oh. Not very far out of London, Tommy. Far enough though. They certainly made sure of putting a lot of distance between us and a lot of other interests in her way."

"She's probably married one of the London gentry by now."

"Tommy!" The culprit positively blanched under the most pointed maternal stare he had experienced in years.

"I'm sure the girl will be missing you no matter what delights London has to offer. Home is where the heart wants to be."

"If they want me to stay on at Liverpool during the trials it will be well after Nicola's birthday by the time I get back to Newcastle. Her birthday's on the twenty eighth of September and the trials start on the first of October so they can't complain if I go straight round to Jesmond as soon as I get back."

"And what then?"

Fenwick blinked, almost thinking aloud. "If she hasn't come back I don't know what I'll do, but I think she will come back, and when I see her I'll ask her to marry me. In a sense, her father has been right. I know I've had a lot of time to think and I know very clearly how much she means to me. Nothing else is so important. If she can take a chance on me, I know we can be happy together."

Clem tapped his pipe on the grate, clearing his mind at the same time. "You know you'll be asked about your prospects again?"

"Yes, and what's more, I know that Nicola will have seen many big houses and mixed with many more and wealthier people than she ever did in Newcastle. I've seen something of them myself.

I know her father to be a decent man and I've a feeling he has some allowance for me because he has always followed in the wake of his brother and maybe he has depended on family money to get where he has. For me, I'm doing well with the Stephensons and I do share their conviction that there is a big future in railways of one kind or another. Everyone who has worked well with the Stephensons has been looked after and offered some prospect when they needed to change. We just have to look at Matt!"

"Well then, if you're sure you have no problem there, what about religion, your other big hurdle?"

"I'm far from saying I haven't got a problem but I think I could perhaps make reasonable provision for us both. So far as religion is concerned, I do know how important it is to Nicola and how unhappy she would be even to think about a change. She would be a different person if she did. If we get that far, I would change. Her faith means so much to her, perhaps it would be the right thing for me, seeing as how we sail the same tack in so many other directions."

Rosina, who had been absorbed in every word said reflectively, "I can see you've been doing a lot of thinking, Fenwick."

"Never thought so much in my life before. Really, there were times I thought my head would split."

"I hope with all my heart it all comes right for you, I really do. I will say this. I've known some good marriages between couples of different religions, but many more where the differences brought serious trouble. If you really love this girl, Fenwick, my advice would be that you take up her religion."

Clem couldn't resist the thoughtful pause in the discussion. "You never know you know, it might be nice having a papist in the family."

$$- o\ 0\ o -$$

Even in a dismantled state, the *Rocket* comprised some very heavy and fairly cumbersome components, made all the heavier and bulkier by the protective packing to see it safely through its overland journey to Carlisle, its loading and unloading and whatever hazards the sea leg to Liverpool might throw up. The various parts were hoisted and thoroughly secured to a variety of carts hauled by one, two or four horses as the load required. Nothing was left to chance, and anything likely to be needed for the contest was loaded at Forth Banks.

Rumours already abounded of the prospect of underhand dealings or at least the unexplained absence of commonplace materials near the trial site so no risks were to be taken with the running of the *Rocket*.

The impressive caravan headed west out of Newcastle and made good progress. The late summer roads were dry for the most part and the prevailing westerlies would soon dry out whatever rain did fall.

The road itself was of some interest to the military and was kept in passable repair.

That being said, the Newcastle convoy wasn't without difficulties. Weight and bulk presented their own problems and many times Fenwick watched in some mild admiration as the apparently rough and ready teams exercised their mixture of skill, strength and experience to the negotiation of some highway hazard. There was always some narrowing of the road, some inconvenient stone wall, some huge overhanging tree, some awkward bend or dip to get past. This they always did, albeit with customary vociferous mutual instructions and encouragement generously laced with quite unparliamentary language and ancient expletives. Each to his own.

No more difficult than most days, but seemingly longer, were the Tyne and other river crossings. Bridges could be problems, especially those with steep arches or approaches. In the event, though they took time, they proved to be not too difficult and their westwards journeys were always resumed in good order.

To break the monotony, as the occasion presented, Fenwick would ride out if it were not too far and inspect some locally known Roman remains. These were quite varied and usually associated in some way with Hadrian's Wall that was not all that far away. This was an interest of the Rev. Hodgson and Fenwick wondered which of these he had seen.

Carlisle was a welcome sight. It usually is. The road in was mostly level and without problems. The sun was shining as the tired but exuberant Newcastle contingent pulled into the canal basin. There the lighter was waiting to take the dismembered *Rocket* out to a deep-water vessel for shipment to Liverpool. For the stalwarts of our wagon teams it meant the end of two very hard and long days of haulage work, a substantial payout, some decent food and lodgings, and as much beer and other delights as could be found in this fine old border garrison town.

So far, so good.

The wagon drivers and some others were taking an interest in the loading on to the lighter but most of the haulage team had their interest elsewhere it must be said. For Fenwick, the scene brought back many familiar memories. He watched the crane men and slingers as they worked. Like many lowly paid jobs of presumed low skills, slinging is not as easy as it looks. Judgement of balance and support is key. During his early days at sea he had marvelled at the huge loads jerked off the docksides and bound skywards transferring to cavernous ship's holds, all evidently under the supreme orders of the scruffy laughing cavalier beside him, known as a slinger.

He went on board to see the essential components and various stores safely stacked. As he made his way to the stern of the boat, he noticed on the canal side one of the local slingers. It wasn't that he was doing anything wrongly or out of place with his job. He wasn't particularly doing anything. That was it; he didn't seem certain what to do next. He wasn't chatting to his mates. He wasn't whistling. He wasn't smoking, but he was preoccupied with something.

The next item to be loaded was *Rocket's* boiler. If there was one item above all others essential to *Rocket's* success, this was it. All of George's practical judgement and intuition together with Robert's burgeoning design skills were invested in this key piece of advanced engineering. Groundbreaking in concept, producing the reality was a magnificent achievement. The slinger had positioned himself alongside the boiler packing case, marked as such in workmanlike fashion, and was attaching a rope sling to one end of the sturdy wooden base. He then motioned to a fellow slinger to attach a similar rope sling to the other end of the base. As they waited for the crane man to move the jib and hook over the boiler packing case, the slinger who had attracted Fenwick's interest glanced round to the corner of a nearby dockside building.

Fenwick turned and caught sight of a man in the shadow of a gable end. He looked out of place among dockside workers, almost furtive, and clearly not wanting to be noticed. Their eyes met. There was instant recognition. Not a flicker of a doubt either way. Fenwick immediately knew who it was. Frank Whitely for his part, operating for some years now as Robert Smith, never forgot a face. He had good reason to. For keeping one step ahead of the law it was a valuable asset many a time. Whitely's reaction was to get out of sight and get away. Fenwick instinctively knew that his own reaction now could somehow be crucial.

A glance back at the suspiciously acting slinger, now clearly ashen faced and petrified having seen the inexplicable visual exchange, galvanized Fenwick into bellowing at the crane man to stop. He leant over the side of the vessel shouting for the fleeing slinger to be stopped and he charged down the gangplank to get a look at the damage. As feared, one of the slings had been partially severed and would probably have given way after a few moments of lifting. The damage to the Stephensons' advanced piece of boiler technology was beyond thinking about. There would not have been time, even if the facilities could have been found, to carry out repairs or fabricate a replacement in time for the contest. End of the Newcastle entry. End of how much more?

In the instant commotion on the canal side the slinger managed to make his escape before anyone knew what to react to.

"Don't worry about him. He's well enough known around here and the Constable will soon find him. What was he up to?"

Breathing heavily, more in shock than exertion, Fenwick pointed to the cuts in the sling. "I think that tells it all. Could have killed somebody. Never mind the damage to our locomotive."

"The Constable's been called so let's put those slings to one side for him to have a look at and we'll get finished with the loading."

A heavily moustachioed representative of the law very soon did arrive and took extremely detailed notes, showing none of the urgency Fenwick would have wished, and quite reasonably making the most of an out of the ordinary call on his services. One could not be too careful taking names and details in these cases. One never knew which superior or which of the Magistrates might show a persistent and penetrating interest. Fenwick did relax a little when he was told the tide would not be a problem to the departure of *The Rocket*.

Although he went as far as to tell the Constable he believed the man by the canal side building was a Robert Smith he had once come across on survey work in the Liverpool hinterland, he didn't declare that this was an alias actually hiding a murder of a few years ago. He genuinely feared that opening up that can of worms at this particular time could well lead to his mission being stopped and Whitely and his sponsors thereby winning anyway.

He was truly relieved when the lighter was allowed to leave, and only relaxed properly when his precious cargo was transferred in its entirety to the deep-sea cargo vessel hove to at Bowness and got under way to the Mersey and Liverpool.

Chapter 11 - Competition and Fanny Kemble

An expectant bustle penetrated every corner of the trial site at Rainhill, nine or ten miles out of Liverpool on the chosen railway route to Manchester. The Railway Company had prepared well, building a large grandstand for the huge numbers of spectators predicted and allocating ample base areas to each of the selected contestants, within convenient distance of the marked double track to be used for the competition.

The gargantuan task of selecting credible entries from the hundreds of applicants from these islands, from continental Europe and America, was carried out by the Company with due fairness but with total regard for its essential commercial interest in the outcome. In the view of some of the newspapers, the competition was a national jamboree to give everyone vaguely interested in transport a once in a lifetime opportunity to publicise and try out his pet ideas in the spotlight of this unique national stage.

The Company wasn't doing this for fun. It wanted clarity that locomotives could reliably do what was being claimed for them. If they could, then several key issues in the design of their Liverpool to Manchester railroad would be resolved.

A firm line was taken with ideas from crackpots and the legions fascinated with theories and plans for perpetual motion. Many credible scientists and engineers had spent time getting nowhere much with perpetual motion and the company did not intend to spend its capital pursuing such speculative ventures.

Eliminating the impossibles and the improbables had a dramatic effect on the tatterdemalion list of aspiring contenders. Those others that would need some serious financial investment, engineering resources and time for development were similarly discarded. There were also some genuine and recognised potential combatants who did not enter, for lack of interest or other reasons.

At the end of this process the Company decided to seek out the most improved engine based on present working knowledge and to put five to the test.

1. *The Novelty*
2. *The Sans Pareil*
3. *The Rocket*
4. *The Cycloped*
5. *The Perseverance*

The Rainhill trial was rapidly becoming something of a horse race in the opinion of the public, and certainly in the newspapers. In those terms the first three were the recognised front-runners, number four would be an 'also ran', and number five an outsider.

Fenwick's worry had always been Timothy Hackworth's *Sans Pareil*. He had seen it under construction down at Shildon in County Durham; he knew Timothy's abilities and the machine he was entering looked formidable and businesslike. Then, out of nowhere it seemed, came *The Novelty*. Light in comparison with either of the entrants by the two northern constructors, it looked like a racer and rapidly became the popular favourite.

The Stephensons quietly set about arranging their base, the two forever in close conversations. Robert, who had designed *The Rocket*, meticulously supervised its reassembly and George's eye took in all of the preparations for the coming contest. They were both wholly focussed on the importance of succeeding in this ordeal and, in truth, that is what it was. It was a trial of machine against machines, and no simple race. For the crowd, for the newspapers, it might be an exciting and colourful spectacle but for the makers of the locomotives it was very much more than just a race.

"There's a constable to see you, Fenwick."

Ignoring the ribald suggestions that everyone around seemed unable to resist offering, Fenwick strained to take in the rest of the message.

"It's about the Carlisle business, he's over there."

He'd been provided with one of the light wooden chairs in the temporary construction designated as the Newcastle base, and was already licking his pencil, notebook at the ready, as Fenwick arrived. The law's bulky local custodian looked up as his quarry appeared.

He then stood up, which was just as well because one of the back legs of his relatively miniscule chair was sinking into the yet untrodden grass under the canvas awning. Indignity might soon have followed imbalance.

"Are you Mr. Fenwick Skipsey?"

"Yes."

"I've been asked to inform you of matters pertaining to the felony in Carlisle docks which involved you and Mr. Stephenson's locomotive and others."

"Thank you." Fenwick wasn't sure what else to say and was wondering what was coming next.

"We have apprehended a dock labourer and he has been charged with causing malicious damage to company property. The charges can't be more serious because, fortunately, he did not succeed in his apparent intentions. At Carlisle, they were unable to take matters further as the man claimed not to know the name of the person who had persuaded him to interfere with the slings. He also claimed not to know anything about the particular container pointed out to him.

Now, the name I understand you gave to the Constable at Carlisle, Mr. Robert Smith. Is that so?"

"Yes." Fenwick couldn't but answer otherwise, yet had a sinking feeling that he might be getting into hotter water than would be comfortable.

"The name is common enough," went on the Constable, "but to our people in the Carlisle area there was no one of that name, to their knowledge, who was likely to be involved in that kind of activity." He paused for breath, and focussed intently on the face in front of him. Their Report says that you had some time previous, come across this man in the Liverpool area? Where and when was that, might I ask?"

Fenwick outlined the experience of his survey work with Matt. With his heart in his mouth, he avoided saying that he had not actually come face to face with Smith, and was more than a little relieved that his interrogator did not pick up on this point. He hadn't thought the matter through, and once again, didn't want at this particular time to get involved in enquiries that might take him out of the Rainhill efforts.

Perhaps the Constable's next line of thought was distracting him from questioning Fenwick's narrative in closer detail. "Here in Liverpool, the name may mean something more to us. I can't say anything at this stage but we do have knowledge of at least one individual we wish to trace and question. He came to these parts some years back from the West Yorkshire House of Correction at Wakefield. Does that mean anything to you?"

As calmly as he could, Fenwick shook his head. Wakefield sounded ominously on some sort of route; it chilled him to think, from east Lincolnshire to Tyneside.

"One other matter. You may not know about yet. One of your adversary locomotives has been overturned in transit and may be damaged. Mr. Burstall's *Perseverance* from Edinburgh. I informed the two Mr. Stephensons of this occurrence when I arrived enquiring for you. Do you think that this matter could be linked to the attempt on the Stephenson locomotive at Carlisle?"

Once again Fenwick felt the calmly penetrating eyes appearing to read his mind. This time it was much easier to say no.

- 0 O 0 -

The Rocket was steamed up and ready to go, George Stephenson at the controls. It was still early morning but there were things to do. Typically but not predictably, Stephenson had arranged to attach an open but comfortably furnished passenger carriage to *Rocket*. Off he went, also as previously arranged, to pick up for a private and exclusive demonstration run the worthy Directors of the host Liverpool & Manchester Railway Company.

These gentry were in great good humour, almost to a man. White ribbons in buttonholes. No pressing business to discuss, they were here to relax and enjoy the day. It was their day. For the time being the boardroom debates were over, Company decisions were all postponed. They chatted and joked, revelling in their own company, conversation rambling without pause in a jolly atmosphere not usually engendered without a good dinner and unlimited champagne. They knew, contentedly and beyond doubt, that this event and their Company were at the centre of the nation's attention. Indeed it went wider. The applied scientific and engineering brains of all of Europe and America were aware of the Rainhill Locomotive Trials and watching.

Thousands of people in the flesh were here to watch, the grandstand filling. Hundreds of company employees, not to mention the Special Constables, were arranged to marshal the crowds and, in particular, to keep them off the double tracks and to the grandstand side of them. The opening day was an opportunity for the competitors and the judges to familiarise themselves with the terrain and the facilities the Company had provided for each of them. Equally, it was an opportunity for the Directors, the scientific community, the press and the public to have a close look at the best our nation's engineers could come up with.

The noise from the crowd in the grandstand was all of animated and cheerful argument. Everyone had a favourite, all had an opinion and, unless side bets had been placed, no one had directly anything to lose whatever the outcome. Everyone was an authority on some aspect. No one could yet be shown wrong with certainty. Every feature of the competing machines was appraised and discussed at length. Every scientist or would-be authority of whatever relevance pronounced from on high. Every facet and attribute was analysed and dissected. Dr. Dionysius Lardner and his ilk had many a field day.

In her striking yellow and black livery, with an unusual white shining smokestack, the *Rocket* set off, George Stephenson standing tall and composed at the controls. Not at all heavily loaded, she was soon up to speed and breezily flying off in the direction of Rainhill; smoke blowing overhead and steam swirling past driver and passengers. The sensation was unreal. Even Directors were not used to travelling at such speeds. The recently laid rails for the new railway were impressively smooth and the chosen two-mile straight and level ideal for the purpose of the competition.

Nearing the level was the much-debated Rainhill incline. Too steep for locomotives insisted many. Fixed engine houses and hauling ropes would be needed here and at many other inclines. George Stephenson would have none of this argument. Locomotives must not be strangled by ropes. *Rocket* stormed up the long steady slope and settled that argument visibly, once and for all.

Reaching the start of the level and gliding onwards past the grandstand to the end of the two-mile stretch, Stephenson brought them to a smooth and steamy halt. Smiling at his guests, and confident that one fundamental design argument had already been won he was delighted to see them happily enervated with the novel experience of comfortable speed and the rush of the morning air. The frequent clouds of steam, the occasional wafts of smoke and the sporadic airborne hot cinder from the furnace smokestack appeared to concern them not a jot. Glancing backover past their minor forest of top hats, he changed grip to the regulator and reversing lever to bring them bowling in fine style whence they came. This further short run brought them to within a short distance of their Company's marquee. An experience to savour and hopefully a favourable association and start for Tyneside's *Rocket*.

"Take her back and check her over, Bob."

The Stephensons got down from the *Rocket* and walked with the Directors over to the Railway Company's exclusive encampment. This was some little distance from the impressive grandstand and the comfortably appointed further marquee provided for the ladies. Huge areas were already taken with carriages, traps and drays of all descriptions, their resettling horses, drivers and attendants.

Bob M'Cree, an experienced locomotive driver, brought *Rocket* back to its base while the Stephensons took note of the precise conditions of the exacting trial which would commence in earnest the following day.

"Fenwick, Jed, we should lead some water, coal and coke, and a few other bits and pieces to the other end of the two mile stretch in case of emergencies. There's talk of a lot of non-stop runs up and down to make the trial like an unbroken journey from Liverpool to Manchester, or back again." Jedediah Brown was a stolid, apparently uncomplicated Northumbrian who had been in George Stephenson's employ for many a year. Apart from an ability to turn his hand to just about any skill needed in the workshop, he was totally trustworthy and possessed an almost uncanny knack of anticipating troubles. Very much a man after George's own heart and very much valued by him. He and Fenwick had struck up a friendship.

They were discussing what items to have on standby at the end of the measured run when there was a roar of approval and anticipation from the grandstand.

"The *Novelty*'s coming out!"

Indeed it was. Resplendent in Royal Blue, low, light and racy, its copper boiler shining in the mid-morning sun it looked every bit the new modern speedster. The crowd cheered its appearance in both meanings of the word. So this was what new design could mean.

Almost half the weight of the two northeast entrants, the *Novelty* was neatly engineered, impeccably turned out and evidently capable of being driven by gentlemen at leisure.

It rapidly gained speed and shot past the grandstand with a nonchalance that belied its velocity. Its low profile and its slender outline made it look all the faster.

The waving and cheering of the crowd demonstrated its reassurance in its choice of favourite and the enjoyment of seeing it so dramatically in action. The build-up to the event had been right. The opinions of those who should know these things had been vindicated. The formidable engineering partnership of Braithwaite and Ericsson had indeed produced the goods. The beautiful, light and elegant *Novelty* hadn't come all the way from London just to make up the numbers.

Truth to be told, it had been an achievement for Braithwaite and Ericsson to get their machine to the starting line. The competition had been drawn to their attention rather late in the day. Their engineering pedigree was not in heavyweight colliery locomotives and there were no lengths of rails in London to do any useful tests on. Nevertheless, their distinctive design was very much up and running, and at Rainhill. At the end of one run there was a minor explosion followed by vivid sparks. It could also be seen that water was pouring from a joint and the sleek burnished locomotive was driven hastily to its base for examination and repair. Teething troubles, no doubt.

"That was a lot faster than *Rocket*, Jed."

"Aye. Credit where it's due."

"I wonder what George and Robert are thinking? If I'm any judge, that must have been over twenty-five miles an hour. It doesn't seem all that long since we all had to keep quiet about speeds only half that. Frighten the horses and womenfolk would it? There's horses and two-legged fillies all over here and not one of them seems bothered."

"Perhaps George won't be all that bothered either. He was taking it easy, first thing this morning. Tomorrow'll be different. The engines will have a load to pull and yon won't get far on the few baskets of coals it carries on the deck. It might just have enough water underneath, Fenwick, but think on, it has no tender at all."

"What's up?"

The noise from the grandstand had fallen to a steady anticipatory hum, but now a gleeful roar erupted. Was it cheering or jeering? Hard to tell. Perhaps it was large and enthusiastic measures of both.

Cycloped by Mr. Brandreth of Liverpool had entered the lists. As unlike any of its fellow competitors as it was possible to imagine, it lumbered unsteadily into view, more wood than metal, and powered by age-old horse rather than relatively new steam. Even so, it was a lot heavier than *Novelty*. Its basic design was a moving endless belt walkway. A horse or a pair of horses caused the walkway to move and this movement was transmitted to wheels on the rails below. The essential principle was that of the prison treadmill or the wheel driven from the inside by dogs or other small animals.

Encouraged by the enthusiasm of the crowd, *Cycloped* trundled slowly and heavily past the grandstand and back again to generous applause. In a practical sense it worked. Its speed, however, was no more than that of its driving force, the horse. It might have its uses, but leading large loads of goods and passengers all the way from Liverpool to Manchester wouldn't be one of them. A good try, Mr. Thomas Shaw Brandreth even if one of your horses hadn't put its foot through the floor, but now do let us get on with the serious competitors, was the general feeling.

"What on God's earth is that doing here?"

"Well, Mr. Brandreth is a Director of the Railway Company and a Barrister. Perhaps he called in a few favours from his friends on the Board. I don't know. Anyway, what are you complaining about, Jed? It must have been let in for some light relief! What else, eh?"

The *Sans Pareil* was a different kettle of fish altogether. If the popular opinion was that the Stephenson locomotive was heavy and unrefined in comparison with the London favourite, Timothy Hackworth's entry confirmed their view that these scaled down colliery workhorses were history. Fine for pulling prodigious loads of coal to the collier vessels, but not for general merchandise, and certainly not for passengers. Far too heavy and smoky.

Timothy Hackworth had worked manfully to produce and prepare *Sans Pareil* for this contest. Although he had the facilities of the Stockton & Darlington Railway to work with, his design and production had almost all to be carried out in his own time and at his own expense. His competition locomotive clearly was a scaled down version of his successful working designs reliably operating for a number of years in the northeast. It was heavy though, the heaviest of the five competitors.

In her green, yellow and black livery she made a formidable sight as Timothy set off along the two-mile straight. She was no slouch either. Her speed was more than adequate to the needs of the Directors and to the benchmarks of the judges. In one criterion she might be lacking. She was producing more red-hot cinders from her smoke stack than would be acceptable. More objectionable than *Rocket's* initial black smoke and a lot more than anything coming from *Novelty*. Perhaps the starting up from cold coal fires was the problem and later running on coke the answer.

The three main contenders appeared at various times throughout the afternoon, then resorting to their bases for water or fuel, adjustments or repairs as necessary. It was well into the afternoon that the final competitor made its appearance. Not exactly the pride of Scotland, and having some passing similarities with the London entry, the vividly red-wheeled *Perseverance* from Edinburgh came out to show its paces. Its paces were not all that brisk. Its design sprang from steam road carriages like *Novelty* and had a vertical boiler set in a short flat deck. There the similarities ended. The heavy central boiler dominated the design and gave no redeeming character. It wasn't too difficult to imagine this machine toppling over from its wagon on the road down from Edinburgh to Liverpool.

Mr. Burstall put his protégé through its paces, and very noisy paces they were. He had also been working manfully on repairing his damaged machine ever since they got to Liverpool. Wherever the problems came from; basic design, initial build, or hasty repairs, it was clear that the six miles per hour or so that *Perseverance* struggled to manage could only provide competition for *Cycloped* and not the three main contenders. The grandstand exuded patience rather than appreciation as the Scottish entrant made its laboured way up and down.

"Did you ever hear a racket like that? Every nut and bolt must have had bags of room to move about, and perhaps those red wheels were nearer square than round. They should have invited the Gateshead lads to bring *Chittaprat.* Then we could have had a competition for the noisiest locomotive in the kingdom."

"Were you there the day yon Burstall showed up at Newcastle?"

"Oh yes, Jed. I'd almost forgotten. It was quite a while before anyone realised who it was and why he might be looking about our workshops."

"Well he couldn't have learnt much from us on this showing. Not that our secrets are proper secrets mind."

Fenwick was feeling just a little more relieved now that the *Perseverance* from over the border was no longer an unknown outsider. On what he had seen so far, the Ordeal would be between their *Rocket,* Timothy Hackworth's *Sans Pareil,* and the favourite from London, Braithwaite and Ericsson's sleek *Novelty.*

"I think I might know who he talked to."

"Who?"

"One of the men in the foundry, from Byker. He was telling me he had taught his young mate all he knew – 'and he still knows nothin'."

Afternoon tea was being served to the Directors, their ladies and guests. Robert Stephenson came over to the base, almost at a trot. "Bob. Can you get *Rocket* ready for another run. We've a very special guest, Fanny Kemble."

A cannon shell couldn't have caused more consternation. "*The* Fanny Kemble?"

"None other. She's staying in our hotel in Liverpool. She's here for the trials and I can vouch that she's extremely interested in what's going on."

Slightly bewildered minds were trying to focus on the unexpected situation. "Do you want the passenger coach hitched up?"

"No, the *Rocket* and tender will do. In conversation, my father made the offer and she insists on riding the footplate. She's quite determined I can assure you. Get everything as clean as the day it left Newcastle, especially the furnace stays she can hold on to. Put a wooden box in the tender for her to stand on getting up to the footplate, a couple of clean cloths handy, and I'm sure everyone will be on top behaviour. Bob, bring the *Rocket* round to the far end of the grandstand with a full furnace in just about half an hour."

Fanny Kemble was a stunningly beautiful young woman. Intelligent and vivacious, she was a popular favourite of men and women alike. Dark eyebrows and eyelashes set off her attractive features and added an appealing charm to her lively sense of fun. Barely twenty years of age, she was already considered to be the best actress of her generation. Of a theatrical family, her aunt was none other than the celebrated Mrs. Siddons. This had given her an introduction to the theatre, no doubt, but her evident talent had already secured her place as a top-level actress. There was an eager anticipation throughout the London theatre world of her forthcoming and most appropriate role of *Juliet* at Covent Garden.

Bob M'Cree alighted from the waiting locomotive as the select little party drew near. The fascination of the grandstand was tangible. Guesses as to the identity of the winsome vision were changed to fascinated understanding as George and Robert Stephenson led their delightful young guest in the direction of *Rocket*. Bob carefully placed an upended and sturdy shallow toolbox alongside *Rocket*'s footplate and gave it a firm shake to make sure it was steady and wouldn't wobble. Standing up, he touched a forelock instinctively, nodded and said, "Ma'am." He was rewarded with a ready smile and an incline of the head he thought would leave him melted forever.

George released Fanny's arm to Robert's and stepped first up onto the footplate with an agility designed to minimise the near thirty years between himself and his young charge. Reaching down, he then took one hand as she gathered her skirts with the other, and saw her safely alongside him on the adequate but sparse metal footplate. "Hold tight to yon bar with your left hand young lady. Your right hand might have to choose between that bonny hat and me as we get up some speed."

With smiles and waves from them both, he slowly opened up the steam valve and they eased away. Away from the waving and well-wishing little sending off party by the side of the track and to the envious cheers of many a young buck in and around the grandstand wishing he was the one with the lovely Frances Ann Kemble.

Hugely anticipating the trip, she felt an immediate affection for the compact and busy *Rocket*. With a roaring fuss of steam to left and right it glides off eager to get on its way, soon flying like a bird and rhythmically breathing white steam. Better not try to pat it. That's a fiercely hot furnace and some of these pipes must be scalding. Fields and hedges are flying by, miniature people in the distance waving. I'm on a magic metal carpet speeding to the ends of the earth. My bonnet very soon needed to be taken off and clasped in front of me. The wind flattens my cheeks, flows over my face and ripples through my hair. Eyes forced closed under the lids, it's spellbinding, and I'm flying, flying.

And this man beside me. I've quite fallen for him, I really have. Never heard this soft distinctive Northumbrian voice before. So thoughtful and gentle a man, with his mature kindly face yet strikingly in charge of this new world. A world of movement and speed. A world of new devices, new experiences and smells. Of hot steam and oil and roaring furnaces. I think I'm intoxicated.

George smiled to himself at the rapt smile on the young face beside him, eyes closed, and who knows what thoughts passing. Having reassured himself of her safe serene, even confident, poise on the footplate beside him, he responded to her initial bright questioning chatter then left the experience to speak for itself. It was also an experience for himself. In the exclusive company of this exquisite young woman, so extraordinarily well thought of at the highest levels of society, he relaxed to her unaffected charm in an easy contentment he had rarely known.

On the return journey he could not resist opening *Rocket*'s throttle in a final exhilarating burst of speed. The years slipped off his squared shoulders, the smile on his face he knew was just as broad. The sun shone. He stood taller than when they had set off such a little while ago. The world felt good. Perhaps, after all, there might just be something to be said for that vexatious and strangely spoken tribe from the south.

Chapter 12 - Triumph at Rainhill

The Judges were out smart and early. White marker posts had been set alongside the railway track, one and a half miles apart, the distance meticulously measured, checked and checked again. At each end of the measured trial distance an overrun of a quarter of a mile was allowed for getting up to speed or stopping. At one end there were repair facilities for the use of all of the competitors, a blacksmith's shop and a weighbridge. At both ends there were supplies of water, coal and coke, all to be equally meticulously dispensed to each of the competitors prior to starting up, closely supervised, and from cold.

Chosen by the Company Directors for their knowledge of the subject and for their impartiality, the Judges would not have laid claim to the Wisdom of Solomon but to a man they were determined to attempt his even-handed fairness. They would note the time taken to get up to steam, the time taken to turn about, and the total amount of fuel and water used. Speed and economy were of crucial interest to the Company. They knew full well how much hung in the balance for the successful locomotive maker. Notebooks, watches with seconds hands, and spare watches with seconds hands at the ready then.

Each locomotive would be required to pull three times its own weight and to make twenty double runs over the course. An interval would be allowed after ten such flying runs and the total distance covered would be seen to replicate an actual journey from Liverpool to Manchester, and back.

Cycloped had been withdrawn, as anticipated, and with good grace. The Rainhill ordeal was also proving too much of an ordeal for Mr. Burstall and his *Perseverance*. He came to the conclusion that the many repairs he had been obliged to carry out on his machine would still not leave him as a serious competitor to the three principals. He had neither the speed nor the pulling power, so he also withdrew.

For the three remaining champions, the first part of the ordeal was the weighbridge. No problem for *Novelty*, which was self-evidently light. No real problem either for *Rocket* which came comfortably under the prescribed weight, although a tad heavier than had been Robert Stephenson's calculation. For Timothy Hackworth, however, there was true consternation. The *Sans Pareil*, like its two remaining adversaries, was mounted on four wheels. Its measured weight was well over the weight limit for four wheels and it should have been provided with six.

"I've never seen Timothy in such a strop."
"Timothy Hackworth?"

"Yes. Over at the weighbridge. We came in nicely under the limit but his *Sans Pareil* was well over. He went berserk, wouldn't accept it. Said there must be some fault in the weighing mechanism."

"So they're out?"

"Well no. The Judges decided to let them continue but insisted there was nothing wrong with the weighbridge."

"He must have been distraught at having come this far, put in all that effort, and almost not allowed even to start."

"Rules are rules, Jed. Robert Stephenson was a bit surprised *Rocket* weighed in heavier than he expected but at least we didn't face being disqualified before we've even started the trials."

"I've known Timothy a lot of years. Knows his own mind and doesn't easily give way, but for him to be in a temper, there must have been something going on. When I came over here this morning, one of his lads said they'd been working all night on the leaks they got yesterday. Even then, he found time to go over to the *Novelty* camp to offer his help with their problems. They had water leaks all over and to cap it all, the bellows went an' burst. That was the explosion we saw, when they pushed it to the blacksmiths."

"That's typical from what I've heard of him. Strong Methodist or Wesleyan isn't he? Travels miles preaching. Left Wylam after building *Puffing Billy* because he wouldn't work on a Sunday! Doesn't drink, but dead keen on dancing! How does that fit in? And I believe he has almost enough daughters back home to do their own eightsome reels!"

"If you ever need help, Fenwick, he's a man to turn to."

"He really went on at the Judges. Said his machine had its weight spread evenly over its four wheels and *Rocket*'s weight was mostly over its front two. Argued that we'd do more damage to the track, which was the whole point of having a weight limit in the first place."

"Well, at least he can run. Doubtless, *Novelty* had no weight troubles?"

"No, none. Hey up. Action stations. Here comes Robert."

"G'morning. We are to go first. As you know, *Rocket*'s been fired up from cold under the Judges supervision. Once she's up to pressure we're off. You all know your jobs and how important all this is."

There was mounting satisfaction in the Newcastle camp. Hauling the stipulated three times its own weight of freight cars and stones almost as if it wasn't there, *Rocket* tackled the sixty miles of calculated ordeal with a gusto. Forwards and back. Forwards and back. Up and down past the packed, waving and cheering grandstand. Past the pennants and ribbons, the flags and flagpoles. Past the ten, fifteen thousand or more fascinated spectators and the lines upon lines of carriages bordering the twin tracks. Past the enthralled gathering of top hats and cloth caps, of parasols, brightly coloured dresses and more sober Sunday best. They had been taking up position since early morning, all certain of enjoying a momentous occasion, brass bands were playing, and many in the crowd sensed unique history in the air.

Hotels in Liverpool long since sold out, there were encampments in spare farm rooms and in spare farm buildings or simply on farmland for miles around. The highly enterprising landlady of the Rail-road Tavern at nearby Kenwick's Cross must have made her fortune from her boiled beef and roast mutton and her room reserved for 'a better class of visitors'.

The Trials had caught the national imagination with a vengeance. This was a true contest, bare knuckles in the afternoon, oars straining through the cold water, thoroughbreds and thudding flying hooves over the firm turf. May the best man or best horse win, then all salute the hero of the latest hour.

All sections of the populace, all manners of engineer, were caught up with a massive interest in the event, the machines, the occasion.

Rocket ate up the miles, always a touch faster going forward than on the return. Perhaps a psychological caution exerted itself when *Rocket* and driver were pushing rather than pulling the weighted cars. Perhaps the energetic pistons felt happier driving forwards. There wasn't much in it. Up and down the measured track they went, speeding through the marker flags, braking to a halt in the overlap distance allowed and with scarcely a pause for effecting the reverse.

Half the distance covered now. Bring her to a halt. Take more coke onto the tender. Not rationed, but scrupulously measured. Oil-can attention all round. More water. Also by the Judges' strict measure. Nothing so far overheating? Right. How are we doing? No leaks to be seen? Furnace good and level? Pressure O.K. Judges all happy? Let's be on our way again, then. So far so good.

The *Rocket* could do this all day, and George and Robert knew it. Sound as a pound. Charging up and down the familiar track, smoke trails flying, steam exhaust purposefully and rhythmically blowing, their prized yellow and black locomotive must be making an impressive sight. Every run at full load and taken at speeds well over the essential. With the end of the Trial in prospect, and noting full pressure still available, George Stephenson opened up the regulator and accelerated still faster. In full flow, *Rocket* sped imperiously past the grandstand, her ordeal now completed, and hurtling for the eastern final marker post. Stopwatches were noted and readings compared.

Let the doubters doubt. Let the sceptics contrive their reservations. The Stephenson locomotive is clearly up to the job, and more. It has pulled the specified load at up to three times the specified speed, no less. One down, two to go!

"*Sans Pareil* is goin' next. Did you hear what happened earlier? When they were runnin' the locomotive oot, one of the Shildon lads slipped and fell between the rails. Didn't have time to get oot of the way."

"Nivvor in the world!"

"He lay flat, kept his head doon and *Sans Pareil* went clean ower the top of him. Got up, not so much as a scratch".

"Whey y'nivvor! Who was it?"

"Dunno. Might have been that big ginger-haired lad."

"Just as well it wasn't the *Novelty*. Not much room under the fancy London design for that sort of caper."

"I'll bet Timothy was havin' kittens. Aal the effort to get this far and then have to pull oot at the last minute."

"Would he have done that?"

"I'd bet money on it. If there had been a serious injury or, God forbid, a fatality then Timothy would have scratched oot of respect. He's such a strong chapel man, he wouldn't have thought twice aboot droppin' oot of the contest. Wouldn't be the forst time his principles cost him money."

"Nivvor mind. He's on his way the noo. Him and Tammy Grey at the reg'lator."

There was certainly something impressive about *Sans Pareil*. Bigger and heavier than *Rocket*, it clearly came from the same northern background and origins. More a compact, shortened version of Timothy Hackworth's very successfully operating Stockton locomotives, it left the spectators in no doubt that it would be up to the job of hauling the Company's nominated load. In no visible fashion did it have any novelties to match *Novelty* itself, which was clearly of a different species.

The Company had declared its interest in finding the most improved locomotive that today's engineers could produce. Did the Stephensons' specially produced *Rocket* answer? Was *Sans Pareil* the safe sensible choice based on known experience? Should they look to the alternative locomotive evolution represented by the interesting and attractive *Novelty* coming out of road carriage experience?

Sans Pareil was out to make its claim and settle the conundrum for them. With as much indignation in his veins as his locomotive had hot cinders cascading from its black smoking stack, Timothy Hackworth opened up the regulator and charged past the grandstand. Up all night with his team tackling leaks and still smarting from the skirmish at the weighbridge, there was almost a further, final and conclusive last-minute catastrophe.

Having succeeded in stopping the leaks and testing up to pressure, the boiler was still hot when he came up to start the ordeal. The Judges pointed out that this contravened the rules. The locomotive's boiler should start from cold. After some deliberation, the Judges decided to waive that requirement and allow *Sans Pareil* to go ahead and compete.

Compete she certainly did. Standing tall and compact from the rails, a formidable assembly of purposeful and weighty metal, *Sans Pareil* roared off on its task. The big machine sped on its way with an alacrity that belied its appearance and confounded more than a few spectators. Game definitely on. Surely *Rocket* was no faster than this? The load fastened behind seemed to follow as an afterthought. No difficulties there. Perhaps the Directors had miscalculated the load to be pulled in this ordeal? Neither Hackworth nor the Stephensons would have fretted at being asked to haul more.

Forwards and back along the measured miles, reversing with skill and taking on supplies from his willing and practised support teams, the pride of Shildon set about its task. In terms of both speed and hauling capacity the spectating witnesses could see that the two northern entrants were something of a match. The more perceptive ones among them could also see that the practical and businesslike competitor now in front of them was taking on more fuel and water than did the Stephenson machine. Everyone could see that the green, yellow and black locomotive now undergoing its trial in front of them had an abundantly effusive smokestack. Spectators either too close or downwind of the tracks were treated to more black smoke than they would have wished. They took what avoiding action they could from the glowing red-hot ash coming at them from the formidable dominating smokestack. How would the Judges regard, let alone measure, the Directors' stipulation that these competing machines must all 'eat their own smoke'? Their problem.

Well into its imposing stride and on its eighth measured run, there was a huge flash of steam from the sturdy machine and it disappeared into a cloud of its own generated vapour. As the dim haze cleared, it was all too apparent that the locomotive had come to a sudden and unexpected halt.

Timothy Hackworth's feelings can only be imagined. With a sickening heart he knew immediately that this really was serious. The boiler feed pump had failed. Not the slightest chance of running repairs here. A major job to be tackled back at the base. He would ask for a delay, certainly until tomorrow, and then a rerun. He brought his team together and set about the sorry task of manhandling *Sans Pareil* back to their base. Honest hands felt sore with the pushing while proud hearts felt sore with the ignominy. Manhandling their prized but lifeless fabrication was bad enough, but for proud locomotive men here in such public view it was heartrending. The grandstand noise subsided to a questioning hum as the cause of the abrupt halt was debated and sympathetic speculation ensued.

The call then went out for *Novelty* to face its required ordeal. The subdued chatter of the crowd changed as the familiar copper and royal blue speedster came from its lair. Expectations rose at the sight of the contrasting design brought out by the highly respected London team. Braithwaite and Ericsson had risen to the railway company's challenge at remarkably short notice it was widely known. Their design came out of their fire engine and road running expertise and owed nothing to the heavy haulage background of the two northern rivals.

Glinting in the sun, the burnished copper of the boiler took the eye and led it along the low business-like layout mounted on racy wheels and a neatly sprung frame. Ahead of the splendid boiler in a neat array were the fuel panniers, the busy pistons, the air bellows nourishing the fire and, finally, an almost delicate short smoke stack. Hidden underneath the deck or platform, between the wheels and almost out of sight, was the water tank.

Being checked out for its ordeal, *Novelty* was almost a greyhound straining on the leash in comparison with its two ultimate adversaries. Needing no following tender to carry its fuel and water, its overall three times load for the trial was very much smaller in comparison with those of *Rocket* and *Sans Pareil* and a major advantage for the London locomotive. Moving to the start of the two-mile straight, her talented designers carried out their final checks. With a nod from the attending Judge by now confident, relaxed and enjoying his role, the impressively turned-out machine moved resolutely off, was swiftly up to speed and through the starter flag on her way.

"What do you think of her, Jed? She was certainly fast in her demonstration runs yesterday."

"She's fast enough all right. An' that little load to pull should be a very big benefit over us. We'll see. Mind you, Fenwick, I did hear George say that in his opinion, 'it has nee guts'. It's like no locomotive I've ever seen before. So light. More of a perambulating tea urn somebody else said."

"I've seen nothing like it."

The mention of perambulating tea urns set Fenwick's mind off at a tangent. He envisioned *Novelty* in an elegant London setting where the kitchen was about a quarter of a mile from the dining room or terrace. Well turned-out gents like the urbane and educated Braithwaite or Ericsson would be hovering around, handing out expensive Ceylon tea and fancy cakes to Nicola. He could clearly see her turning to them, reaching out her hand and accepting the proffered exquisite china with that warm smile he knew so well. The very thought darkened his humour and a minor wave of irritation and frustration swept over him.

The rail he was standing beside got a miniscule kick by way of his vented feelings, but he was at the same time relieved that neither Jed nor anyone else was looking in his direction at the time. The long year of exile was now over. He would go back to Newcastle with the successful or unsuccessful *Rocket* crew and seek out his Nicola. Perhaps she hadn't returned. Perhaps she had embraced a new style of life down in Kensington. Met someone new and more interesting, with very much more to offer her. He physically shuddered at the thought; the persistent nagging thought that had eaten away at him ever since he so bravely, and so foolishly?, had ridden away from her that cold evening a year ago.

With a slight shake of his head at these unsettling and insoluble ruminations, he turned back to the immediate. *Novelty* had completed her first run in effortless style. All who possessed watches were assailed for the time taken over the initial run. Best guesses had to suffice at this distance from the marker flags. The angle at which they were situated from the flags and the moving bodies of spectators in the sight line didn't help either. If anything, she was travelling faster than either *Sans Pareil* or *Rocket*. Perhaps she would have to travel faster than them, just to make up for her extra stops to pick up the fuel she didn't carry because she had no tender. This could be complicated. Doubtless, the Judges had all of this well in mind. Fast speeds over short distances coupled with too many stops and interruptions to take fuel on board would surely reduce her average speed, and increase the total journey time. However, if the *Novelty* were fast enough would that answer for what the Railway Company had in mind?

Conjecture was almost immediately suspended. On only the second run, *Novelty's* boiler blew. Less spectacular than *Sans Pareil's* stoppage, nonetheless it looked ominously terminal. Steam and water poured out from joints and onto the tracks in volumes for all to see. The locomotive crews and competition officials were pretty much aware of the nature and seriousness of the problems the London team had been struggling with, even if the general public were not. Another feared competitor was wheeled off the innocent but unrelenting field of battle. Another crew mortified with the outcome of their efforts. Some of the Judges made their way shortly afterwards to the *Novelty* base and others to the *Sans Pareil*. There was a short discussion with Mr. Ericsson and a longer one with Mr. Hackworth.

"Have you heard? Ericsson has withdrawn. The damage has been too extensive to repair in any reasonable time for them to try again and fulfil the trial. They've withdrawn from the competition and abandoned the £500 premium!"

"Really! George was right then?"

"Seems so. Nothing wrong with its speed. Perhaps not enough metal in it to run up and down all day long pulling wagons and carriages."

"Just leaves us and *Sans Pareil*!"

"Here's Bob M'Cree, at the double. What fettle, Bob? Lost your breath? You shouldn't be running like that at your age."

"We've won, you blithering haddock. We've won!"

Astonished Tyneside cheers broke out and rang over the field of combat to mingle with the cheering and applause now greeting the Judges announcement being delivered in front of the grandstand by loudhailers.

Jumping around like ecstatic and manic Cossacks, they fell about shaking hands and hugging each other in a demented euphoria. This was Trafalgar and Waterloo rolled into one for this industrious crowd and it was quite some time before Bob M'Cree could continue.

"What's happened, Bob?"

"Well, you know that *Novelty* was badly damaged and they decided they couldn't get it repaired in any reasonable time to have another go. *Sans Pareil* might have been got ready in a day or two, and Timothy Hackworth argued with the Judges up hill and down dale that he should be given some extra time.

The Judges seemed to have made their minds up. Perhaps if *Novelty* was also asking for extra time they might have given in – for both of them. As it was, they declared that in consideration of *Sans Pareil*'s weight and fuel consumption, they had seen enough. Only one locomotive had met all the requirements, surpassing most, and had fully completed the ordeal in all its respects. Accordingly, the Newcastle premium engine *Rocket* was declared the winner and awarded the £500 prize. Wonderful or what? George and Robert will be coming over shortly to say a few words and to arrange some sort of a celebration." The cheering resumed, and at some volume and length.

"Fenwick. We've been asked to stay behind a while to clear our stuff from the two terminal areas and see it locked away here at the base. If you go to the far one, I'll see to this one over here. You never know, if George and Robert ever get through taking all those loads of top hats and fancy dresses on demonstration runs we might even get hold of *Rocket* ourselves to bring our things back. Otherwise, I'll just get hold of a horse and dray." Fenwick nodded and set off for the distant terminus.

There wasn't all that much to assemble and bring away. Most of what was lying around were the fuel supplies and water butts belonging to the Railway Company. He had noticed *Rocket* with an empty carriage on its way back to their base and was casting about to check there was nothing of significance being left behind when the locomotive seemed to be setting off again, in his direction. The resourceful Jed had been successful then. The victorious locomotive's day wasn't quite over yet. He would get a ride on it back to base on this famous day.

For the past hour or more at base, everyone had been wreathed in smiles as wide as the Tyne at Shields. It wasn't surprising then as Jed brought *Rocket* to a halt and clambered down, that Fenwick could see that Jed was grinning from ear to ear and back again. "You've got a visitor, Fenwick. She's waiting for you back there." Jed continued grinning, enjoying the look of mystification on his friend's face.

"Some of the lads think it's Fanny Kemble's sister, she really is a stunner, but she says her name is Nicola."

Fenwick's mouth fell open in shock. He turned to see but the distance was too great. "Nicola?" It was pointless to question Jed. He wouldn't play this sort of a prank on anyone.

Jed had it all worked out. He'd heard of Fenwick's distorted love life and hoped this development presaged a happy conclusion. He would send his friend back on his own, most impressively arriving in command of the acclaimed *Rocket*.

"I'll finish off here, Fenwick. You take *Rocket* back and see what on earth she wants of an ugly sod like you. Best close your mouth for the flies!"

Fenwick was grinning now and his mind not at all rising to the jibe. Nicola here? Her uncle must have brought her. Back from Kensington? There wasn't enough room in his chest for his lungs to breath and his heart to pound. He shook Jed's hand with his right hand and slapped his shoulder with his left. Stretching up, he was on his way before thinking to check fire or pressure. Both were fine and, although the fire was getting low, it should suffice for the two miles back to base and Nicola.

What would she look like? What changes over the long year? Lots of things to talk about. Lots of people she must have met. Lots of places she must have been to. How changed might she be? Then again there was the harrowing and unrelenting possibility, maybe probability, ever nagging away at the back of his mind that she could be there, waiting for him, on a farewell mission. She'd never just send a cold well-mannered letter. Not her.

Better check the fire. Might need another shovel on. *Rocket* was moving rhythmically now at little more than a walking pace. The floor of the tender was swinging compliantly behind *Rocket's* footplate, both trembling with a tranquil clatter as their wheels rode the joints in the rails below. Fenwick turned, stepping over the moving gap between the footplate and the floor of the tender. As his eyes sought to locate the coal and coke shovel, they widened in alarm to see a man clambering over the back of the tender. The face was not that of an irresponsible friendly intruder. It was Frank Whitely.

Fenwick gasped. If he said anything, it was irrelevant. It was as plain as a pikestaff he was in mortal danger. Whitely, or Smith, was scrambling down the remaining small load of coke backed up against the rear end of the tender. As he restored his balance he picked up the shovel and hurled himself at Fenwick in a mounting fury, his face contorted with focussed venom. Fenwick grabbed at the shaft of the shovel before it could come down on him, twisting to one side in an attempt to avoid being forced back over the hazardous swaying gap behind him.

They grappled desperately, bodies crashing against the sides of the tender, as they stumbled about in a frenzied effort to keep or recover or improve on a precious foothold. Face to face, alternately jowl by jowl, swathed in their collective sweat and hot breath, they battled for the possession or the frustration of the shovel.

Turned completely round and pushed towards the back of the tender, Fenwick trod on some loose coke, lost his balance and his grip. He fell back on the bank of coke, cut, bleeding and defenceless. His arms and legs instinctively scrabbled for leverage against the unstable and shifting coke. In that moment he was as defenceless and as vulnerable as a child. Above him against the soft white and blue of the sky he could see the shovel raised and momentarily motionless, poised to come crashing downwards with all the force Whitely was now free to bring down on him.

He raised his cut and coke encrusted hands above his face in a vain defensive reflex. If the flat of the shovel came down on him could he parry it? If Whitely twisted the shovel and the edge came at him, would it slice through his fingers and his face in an unstoppable painful finish?

It didn't come down. It paused. Then it did come down, but crashed against the coke and the floor beside him. In some way Whitely was spent. His face sagged. His eyes looked at Fenwick but through and beyond him.

"Not your fault," was all his pitched voice said. He moved back, putting one foot on *Rocket*'s footplate, steadied himself with one hand on top of the tender's side, jumped down onto the trackside and was gone.

Exhausted, sore and bewildered, Fenwick hauled himself to his feet. His legs felt taut and unsteady. Was he going to be sick? Whereabouts was he? He put out one supporting hand on the tender's wall. What was ahead on the line? Good God, what next? The urgent need to take some action forced his head to clear. *Rocket* had quite literally gone ahead under her own steam, fortunately keeping to the same modest pace he had set off at. They were nearly back at base. They hadn't passed it.

Robert Stephenson had courteously brought Nicola over from the Railway Company marquee to the Newcastle base and was about to retrace his steps. He and his father were then to escort Fanny Kemble back to the hotel they, and many others attending the Trials, were sharing at Liverpool. Robert had been fascinated to find that they shared with her an acquaintance in his friend and contemporary the remarkable Isambard Kingdom Brunel. They had met at a dinner in London. Isambard had made quite an impression. Robert's attention was suddenly drawn by a sharp-eyed member of the crew to the fact that *Rocket* appeared to be on its way back to base driverless. Incredulity gave way to apprehension as it was realised that some sort of struggle was going on within the tender. By the time *Rocket* drew near, the whole of the workforce had gathered to watch its arrival, mystified by the unconventional departure of some unrecognised individual from the footplate but reassured with the appearance of Fenwick at the regulator.

Fenwick brought the locomotive to a halt, smiling weakly at the relieved but derisive cheer that greeted his arrival. Explanations could wait. Then he saw her. She came running over, not caring, but looking every inch the lady her elegant long dress and short steps would allow. He jumped lightly down from the footplate, dreading that his still shaking legs might give way, and instinctively wiping his hands down the sides of his breeches. She looked a vision in powder blue and pink, her wide-rimmed dark blue and white-ribboned hat hanging back framing her face and upswept hair.

Her bright smile of recognition dimmed a little at his unkempt appearance but swiftly returned to full glow as she established that he was all in one piece.

They clasped each other with eyes shut, in an embrace that excluded the rest of the world. He breathed in her perfume and her powder. She felt his arms tightly around her and the toxic aura of steam, smoke and sweat was heady. He absorbed her bodily warmth and her soft sweet breath on his neck. What else could matter?

From holocaust to triumph.

The End

Acknowledgements

I express my appreciation of the help of Mrs. Joan Hewitt, author and historian, of the Felling Local History Society and for her work 'the Township of Heworth'. Other sources were 'George and Robert Stephenson' by L.T.C. Rolt, 'The Rainhill Story' by Anthony Burton, 'Naval Warfare in the Age of Sail' by Bernard Ireland and 'The Battle of Trafalgar' by Geoffrey Bennett.

My good friend, Tony Birney, also a citizen of The Felling for many years has been of inestimable help with comments, encouragement and proof-reading. Any errors, however, in the use of the wonderful language of Shakespeare and Churchill are solely down to me.

BWH

About the Author

Among other things, Bernard Haugh is an engineer and a family man. Nothing original there then. His experience of these two particular attributes links him and, of course, millions of his fellow countrymen and women in a personal way to most of the quite profound and significant events in our latter history.

He sees in this nation's towering contributions to the world's scientific and social development, the crucial participation and instinctive support of so-called ordinary people in recognizing talent and greatness when it counted.

He has lived in Lincolnshire, on Tyneside, and in Kensington. All featured in this novel.

Printed in the United Kingdom
by Lightning Source UK Ltd.
108975UKS00001B/7-12